"THIS BOOK IS NOT ABOUT HOW TO BE HAPPY OR HOW TO BE POPULAR. IT IS ABOUT HOW TO BE SUCCESSFUL, BUT NOT IN THE WAY MOST PEOPLE USE THE WORD . . . IT IS ABOUT LOVING AND BEING LOVED . . . SAVORING THE BEAUTY OF SUNSETS, THE LEAVES TURNING COLOR, THE RARE MOMENTS OF TRUE HUMAN COMMUNICATION . . ."

—Harold Kushner

Sooner or later, we all start to ask: Is this all there really is? Was there something I was supposed to do with my life? With his special, uplifting wisdom, Rabbi Harold S. Kushner leads us to the real challenge of our lives —to fill every day with one day's worth of meaning, to use every part of our capacity to love, to give and feel, to become good human beings. Rabbi Kushner's reassuring and profound new book is, as Norman Vincent Peale said of the last one, "A book that all humanity needs."

"Rabbi Kushner writes clearly and calmly, making his points with an eclectic range of illustrations—from Goethe, Barbara Tuchman, Sartre, Martin Buber, Gail Sheehy and the film *Casablanca* . . . At a time when most self-help manuals are topical consumer reading, it is refreshing to find one that . . . deals with the timeless."

—*The New York Times*

HAROLD KUSHNER

WHEN ALL YOU'VE EVER WANTED ISN'T ENOUGH

PUBLISHED BY POCKET BOOKS NEW YORK

Song lyric on page 94 © 1965 by Paul Simon. Used by permission.

POCKET BOOKS, a division of Simon & Schuster, Inc.
1230 Avenue of the Americas, New York, N.Y. 10020

Copyright © 1986 by Kushner Enterprises, Inc.

Published by arrangement with the author
Library of Congress Catalog Card Number: 86-1962

ISBN: 0-671-55181-7

First Pocket Books printing May 1987

10 9 8 7 6 5 4 3 2 1

POCKET and colophon are registered trademarks
of Simon & Schuster, Inc.

Cover design by Mike Stromberg

Printed in the U.S.A.

In memory of my parents,
JULIUS KUSHNER (1900–1984) and
SARAH HARTMAN KUSHNER (1905–1976),
who live on

Acknowledgments

It seems a long time ago that I first sat down to write this book. I am grateful to my immensely capable editor, Arthur H. Samuelson, who had worked with me on my previous book, for guiding me through the process, for helping me understand exactly what kind of book I was trying to write, and for making sure that I wrote it. My thanks to James Silberman, publisher of Summit Books, for his faith in me and for his insistence that I keep at the project until I had written a book that we could all be pleased with. A word of thanks as well to the members of my congregation at Temple Israel of Natick, Massachusetts, for sharing their lives, their fears, their concerns with me, and to my friends who persuaded me to read the spiritual-psychological writings of Carl Jung. And a very special last word of appreciation to my wife, Suzette, whose optimism and encouragement kept me going even when my own faltered.

HAROLD S. KUSHNER

Contents

About a third of my cases are suffering from no clinically defineable neurosis, but from the senselessness and emptiness of their lives. This can be described as the general neurosis of our time.

—Carl Jung
Modern Man in Search of a Soul

Utter futility, all is futility.

—Ecclesiastes 1:1

ONE

—⊰∞⊱—

Was There Something I Was Supposed to Do with My Life?

A SK the average person which is more important to him, making money or being devoted to his family, and virtually everyone will answer *family* without hesitation. But watch how the average person actually lives out his life. See where he really invests his time and energy, and he will give away the fact that he does not really live by what he says he believes. He has let himself be persuaded that if he leaves for work earlier in the morning and comes home more tired at night, he is proving how devoted he is to his family by expending himself to provide them with all the things they have seen advertised.

Ask the average person which means more to her, the approval of strangers or the affection of people closest to her, and she won't be able to understand why you would even ask such a question. Obviously, nothing means more to her than her family and her closest friends. Yet how many of us have embarrassed our children or squelched their spontaneity, for fear of what neighbors or strangers might think? How often have we poured out our anger on those closest to us because we had a hard day at work or someone else did something to upset us? And how many of us have let ourselves become irritable with our families because we were dieting to make ourselves look more attractive to people who do not know us well enough to see beyond appearances?

Ask the average person what he wants out of life, and he will probably reply, "All I want is to be happy." And I believe him. I believe that most people want to be happy. I believe that they work hard at making themselves happy. They buy books, attend classes, change their lifestyles, in an ongoing effort to find that elusive quality, happiness. But in spite of all that, I suspect that most people most of the time do not feel happy.

Why should that sense of happiness be so elusive, eluding both those people who get what they want in life and those who don't ? Why should people with so many reasons to be happy feel so acutely that something is missing from their lives? Are we asking too much of life when we say, "All I want is to be happy"? Is happiness, like eternal youth or perpetual motion, a goal that we are not meant to reach, no matter how hard we work for it? Or is it possible for people to be happy, but we are going about it in the wrong way?

Oscar Wilde once wrote, "In this world there are only two tragedies. One is not getting what one wants, and the other is getting it." He was trying to warn us that no matter how hard we work at being successful, success won't satisfy us. By the time we get there, having sacrificed so much on the altar of being successful, we will realize that success was not what we wanted. People who have money and power know something that you and I do not know and might not believe even when we are told. Money and power do not satisfy that unnameable hunger in the soul. Even the rich and powerful find themselves yearning for something more. We read about the family problems of the rich and famous, we see their fictionalized conflicts on television, but we never get the message. We keep thinking that if we had what they have, we would be happy. No matter how hard we work at being popular and no matter how good we are at it, we never seem to reach the point where we can relax and feel we have arrived. If our sense of who we are depends on popularity and other people's opinions of us, we will always be dependent on those other people. On any day, they have the power to pull the rug out from under us.

I remember reading of a young man who left home to find fame and fortune in Hollywood. He had three dreams when he set out—to see his name in lights, to own a Rolls-Royce, and to marry a beauty contest winner. By the time he was thirty, he had done all three, and he was a deeply depressed young man, unable to work creatively anymore despite (or perhaps because of) the fact that all of his dreams had come true. By thirty, he had run out of goals. What was there for him to do with the rest of his life?

Several recent authors have written of "the imposter phenomenon," describing the feeling of many apparently successful people that their success is undeserved and that one day people will unmask them for the frauds they are. For all the outward trappings of success, they feel hollow inside. They can never rest and enjoy their accomplishments. They need one new success after another. They need constant reassurance from the people around them to still the voice inside them that keeps saying, If other people knew you the way I know you, they would know what a phony you are.

So, the woman who dreamed of marrying a successful

doctor or corporate executive and living in a fancy house in the suburbs may find herself well married and living in her dream house but cannot understand why she goes around every morning saying to herself, Is this all there is to life? There has to be something more. She makes lunch dates with friends, works to raise money for charity, perhaps opens a boutique, hoping that if she fills her days, she will also fill the gnawing emptiness in her soul. But no matter how busy she keeps herself, the hunger within her is never sated.

Our souls are not hungry for fame, comfort, wealth, or power. Those rewards create almost as many problems as they solve. Our souls are hungry for meaning, for the sense that we have figured out how to live so that our lives matter, so that the world will be at least a little bit different for our having passed through it.

I was reading Carl Jung's book *Modern Man in Search of a Soul* one day, when I came across several passages which startled me with their insight. They gave me the feeling that a man who lived before I was born knew me better than I knew myself. The first passage was, "About a third of my cases are suffering from no clinically defineable neurosis, but from the senselessness and emptiness of their lives. This can be described as the general neurosis of our time."

I had to admit that he was right. He was right about the 1980s as surely as he was about the 1920s and 1930s when he wrote those lines. What frustrates us and robs our lives of joy is this absence of meaning. Our lives go on day after day. They may be successful or unsuccessful, full of pleasure or full of worry. But do they *mean* anything?

Is there anything more to life than just being alive— eating, sleeping, working, and having children? Are we no different from insects and animals, except that we are cursed with the ability to ask, What does life mean? and as far as we know, other creatures don't have that problem? It is a hard question to answer, but an even harder one to avoid answering. For a few years, perhaps, we can put off answering it while we are distracted with educational, career, and marriage decisions. In those early decades, other people have more say in our lives than we do. But sooner or later, we will come face to face with the questions, What am I supposed to do with my life? How shall I live so that my life will mean something more than a brief flash of biological existence soon to disappear forever?

The curator of a butterfly museum in South Wales once introduced me to the "moth with no mouth," a species of caterpillar that lays its eggs and then changes into a moth that has no digestive system, no way of taking in food, so that it starves to death in a few hours. Nature has designed this moth to reproduce, to lay eggs and pass on the life of the species. Once it has done that, it has no reason to go on living, so it is programmed to die. Are we like that? Do we live only to produce children, to perpetuate the human race? And having done that, is it our destiny to disappear and make way for the next generation? Or is there a purpose to our existence beyond simply existing? Does our being alive matter? Would our disappearance leave the world poorer, or just less crowded? As Jung correctly understood, these are not abstract questions suitable for cocktail party conversation. They are desperately urgent questions. We will find ourselves sick, lonely, and afraid if we cannot answer them.

A man sat opposite me in my study one evening. He had called me the day before for an appointment, sounding agitated and saying only that he had a religious question to discuss with me. In my line of work, a religious question can mean anything from the issue of why God permits evil to the question of where the parents of the groom stand during a wedding ceremony. After some suitably vague remarks about his childhood and his early religious training, he told me what was on his mind.

"Two weeks ago, for the first time in my life I went to the funeral of a man my own age. I didn't know him well, but we worked together, talked to each other from time to time, had kids about the same age. He died suddenly over the weekend. A bunch of us went to the funeral, each of us thinking, It could just as easily have been me. That was two weeks ago. They have already replaced him at the office. I hear his wife is moving out of state to live with her parents. Two weeks ago he was working fifty feet away from me, and now it's as if he never existed. It's like a rock falling into a pool of water. For a few seconds, it makes ripples in the water, and then the water is the same as it was before, but the rock isn't there anymore. Rabbi, I've hardly slept at all since then. I can't stop thinking that it could happen to me, that one day it *will* happen to me, and a few days later I will be forgotten as if I had never lived. Shouldn't a man's life be more than that?"

If a tree falls in the forest and there is no ear to hear it, does it make a sound? If a person lives and dies and no one notices, if the world continues as it was, was that person ever really alive? I am convinced that it is not the fear of death, of our lives ending, that haunts our sleep so much as the fear that our lives will not have mattered, that as far as the world is concerned, we might as well never have lived. What we miss in our lives, no matter how much we have, is that sense of meaning.

* * *

We may have all the things on our wish list and still feel empty. We may have reached the top of our professions and still feel that something is missing. We may know that friends and acquaintances envy us, and still feel the absence of true contentment in our lives. So perhaps we have turned to therapy to help fill the void and ground our lives in something firm. We may have remembered that the original, literal meaning of the word "psychotherapy" is "the care and cure of souls," and it is precisely our souls that need caring for. I have personally benefited from therapy at times in my life when I was overwhelmed with problems and needed a skilled outside observer to tell me where I was making things harder for myself. I needed to be told that I was avoiding facing certain truths. In addition, I have used the insights of psychology and psychotherapy to inform my sermons and to counsel troubled members of my congregation. I know that therapy has value, and that it has values. But the values of the therapeutic approach tend to be values of adjustment to what is, rather than visions of a world that does not yet exist. A skilled therapist can untangle some of the emotional knots into which we have tied ourselves. He can remove some of the obstacles to our being happy. He can make us less miserable, but he cannot make us happy. At best, he can bring us back to zero from an emotionally negative situation. He can unblock our ability to live meaningfully, but that is as far as he can take us. When members of my congregation come to me with their personal problems, I make sure to tell them that I am not a trained therapist. I can't do a lot of things that a professional therapist can. But I can offer them something that the therapist cannot: a definition of right and wrong living; a freedom to judge their actions and tell them that something is wrong, morally wrong, not just disfunctional, and that another course of action would be better.

There is an old Yiddish saying, "To a worm in horseradish, the whole world is horseradish." That is, if we have never known an alternative, then we assume that the way we are living, with all of its frustrations, is the only way to live. We come to believe that life has always involved traffic jams and air pollution. Psychotherapy can help us face up to the fact that the world we live in is horseradish. It can cure us of unrealistic expectations about the world. It can teach us to adjust to this world and be less frustrated by it. But it cannot whisper to us of a world we have never seen or tasted. Psychology can teach us to be normal, but we must look elsewhere for the help we need to become human.

The question of whether life has meaning, of whether our individual lives make any real difference, is a religious question not because it is about matters of belief or attendance at worship services but because it is about ultimate values and ultimate concerns. It is religious because it is about what is left to deal with when you have learned everything there is to learn and solved all the problems that can be solved. Religion focuses on the difference between human beings and all other species, and on the search for a goal so significant that we make our lives significant by attaching ourselves to it.

America's Declaration of Independence guarantees every one of us the right to the pursuit of happiness. But because the Declaration is a political document and not a religious one, it does not warn us of the frustrations of trying to exercise that right, because the pursuit of happiness is the wrong goal. You don't become happy by pursuing happiness. You become happy by living a life that means something. The happiest people you know are probably not the richest or most famous, probably not the ones who work hardest at being happy by reading the articles and buying the books and latching on to the latest fads. I suspect that the happiest people you know are the ones who work at being kind, helpful, and reliable, and happiness sneaks into their lives while they are busy doing those things. You don't become happy by pursuing happiness. It is always a by-product, never a primary goal. Happiness is a butterfly—the more you chase it, the more it flies away from you and hides. But stop chasing it, put away your net and busy yourself with other, more productive things than the pursuit of personal happiness, and it will sneak up on you from behind and perch on your shoulder.

To cite Jung a second time: "We overlook the essential fact that the achievements which society rewards are won at the cost of a diminution of personality. Many aspects of life which should have been experienced lie in the lumberroom of dusty memories." I looked at that sentence when I had read it and had the feeling of confronting a truth I had always known and had worked hard at not admitting to myself. Only now, in my late forties, was I prepared to face it. Like so many people, I had become very good at certain aspects of my work, but at the cost of distorting my personality. My family, my own sense of wholeness had paid the price, but society at large was so appreciative of the imbalance that I managed not to notice what I was doing. Their applause, their words of praise and appreciation drowned out the still, small voice inside of me which told me that I was leaving something out.

I remembered the countless evenings I let myself be

persuaded that sitting in on a committee meeting (for the third evening that week) was more important than being home with my family and that the committee could not possibly function without me. (Only years later did a clergyman friend tell me, "God may use you but He doesn't need you.") I thought of the times I would schedule a counseling appointment at an hour that was convenient for the caller but that meant my going without dinner. Some years ago, I was invited to address the graduating class of a rabbinic seminary. I told those young people about to embark on careers in the rabbinate, "There will be Friday evenings when you will rush your family through dinner so that you can get to services on time to give a sermon about the Sabbath as uninterrupted family time. There will be days when you will leave a sick child at home or a child studying for a test, while you go to teach religious values to the Temple youth group. There will be Sundays when you will cancel plans for a family picnic to officiate at a funeral, where you will praise the deceased as a man who never let his business interfere with his obligations to his family. And worst of all, you won't even realize what you are doing as you do it."

I remember reading an interview with one of the most successful auto dealers in America, in which he shared the secret of his success: "I treat everybody who walks into my showroom as if he was my best friend. I find out what he's interested in, what he does for a living, and whatever it is, I pretend I'm interested in that and ask him to tell me about it. By the time I'm done, all he wants to do is buy a car from me." I thought to myself, How sad to have to earn your living like that, by pretending to like everyone until you forget what it really feels like genuinely to enjoy someone's company as a friend, not just as a potential customer. Contrived emotion (What am I supposed to feel now?) replaces genuine emotion (How do I really feel about this person?) until the ability to know what you are really feeling disappears. Perhaps this is why there is so much phony conviviality and so little genuine friendship in the lives of American men today.

And worst of all, society applauds this imbalance, honoring us for our financial success, praising us for our self-sacrifice. "The achievements which society rewards are won at the cost of a diminution of personality." Forces in society won't let us become whole people because we are more useful to them when one small part of us is over-developed. Like hunting dogs who have been trained to bring back the game birds in their mouths without taking a bite out of them, we have become useful to society by denying our own healthy instincts.

This book is not about how to be happy or how to be popular. There are a lot of other books to do that. It is about how to be successful, but not in the way most people use that word. What it is really about is how to be human, how to live with the feeling that you are more than a moth that lives for a moment and then disappears. It is about how to know that you have lived as a human being was meant to live, that you have not wasted your life. It is a book about giving your life meaning, feeling that you have used your time on earth well and not wasted it, and that the world will be different for your having passed through it. It is a book written by a man arrived at middle age, telling you some of the things I know now that I wish I had known when I was younger.

My previous book *When Bad Things Happen to Good People* was written to help people cope with the kind of shattering tragedy that divides a person's life in two, before and after that terrible moment. A tragedy like that— the death of someone you love, a crippling accident, or diagnosis of an untreatable illness—concentrates the mind. You cannot help dealing with it, trying to figure out how your life will be different because of it. This book is written to help people cope with another, more subtle kind of tragedy: the disease of boredom, meaninglessness, a sense of the futility and purposelessness of our lives. In some ways, it is a more dangerous problem because we do not always realize that it is happening to us. It has a way of sneaking up on us, draining the joy and zest out of our lives until, when we realize what is happening, it is too late for us to do anything about it. This book tries to help us deal with the fear that we will live and one day we will die, and neither our living nor our dying will make a difference to the world.

I started to write a very different book, a rather detached book about other people's problems, full of advice about how to solve them. I wrote for a while and realized that something was missing. I came to realize that I would have to write this book out of my own problems and confusion, not other people's. I would have to make this a very personal book, as my previous book was, writing not about man's search for meaning in the abstract but about my own search, with all of its mistakes and frustrations.

Three things have happened to me in the last five years which have reshaped the way I look at my life. First, I wrote a book about our fourteen-year-old son's death from an incurable illness, and how I found the resources to accept and survive it. I wrote it out of my own need to tell the story, with no expectation that anyone outside of a small circle of friends would ever read it. To my amazement (and to the amazement of the two publishers who saw it first and turned it down), it became an international best-seller. Years later, I still get letters of appreciation from people who were helped and comforted by it. The book's success brought me some measure of fame and fortune, kept me impossibly busy for several years, put a strain on my health, my family, and my non-book-related activities. But what it did more than anything else was force me to sort out the desirable from the less desirable in all of that glitter. Time and again I had to ask myself, "Is this what I really want out of life?" Sometimes the answer was an emphatic *yes,* sometimes a reluctant *no.* But in either event, I had to face the question with a frequency and urgency I had never known before. I had to decide how I wanted to spend the limited time and energy I had, and what I really wanted to be remembered for. The mistakes I made and the lessons I learned trying to answer those questions are the foundation of this book.

The second thing that happened to me was that my father died just short of his eighty-fourth birthday, forcing me to confront the issue of mortality, his and mine. I had to acknowledge that even the longest and most successful of lives would one day end. I had never known a day of my life without my father there, and now I had to sum up the whole story of his life and see what was left. My father had been a very active, successful man for many years, and now I would see which of all his achievements died and disappeared with him, and which ones remained to give him a measure of immortality. My father's death meant that I was now the oldest generation, the next in line as it were, and it was time to start thinking about what aspects of my own life would outlast me and keep my name and memory alive.

And finally, while I was at work on this book, I turned fifty years old. When I was young, I never dreaded passing my thirtieth or fortieth birthday and no longer being young, as many people do. After all, I come out of a Jewish tradition which reveres wisdom and maturity more than it does the freshness and vigor of youth. I figured forty was a good age for someone who was giving sermons about how to live. But fifty seemed awfully old, distressingly closer to the end of life than to its beginning. Nothing I had ever read prepared me for the surprise of turning fifty. It was so easy. I find myself much more settled, with a much better sense of who I am, than I was at previous milestones. At thirty and even at forty, I had questions about what my life would turn out to be about. At thirty, my wife and I were still in the process of planning our family and having children. I had not yet left the apprentice stage of my career, still serving as assistant rabbi of a large suburban congregation. At thirty-five, I was ambitious and restless, torn between the conflicting claims of my job and my family. At forty, I was struggling against accepting the fact that some of my personal and professional dreams would never come true. I was kicking against life's unfairness, unwilling to accept it. But now I am fifty. Most of the major questions of my life have been answered, some to my satisfaction and some less so. I am confident that there are still surprises ahead of me. I hope I have not stopped growing. But the storms and uncertainties that raged within me when I was younger seem to have calmed.

The need for meaning is not a biological need like the need for food and air. Neither is it a psychological need, like the need for acceptance and self-esteem. It is a religious need, an ultimate thirst of our souls. And so it is to religion that we must now turn to look for answers.

TWO

The Most Dangerous
Book in the Bible

THE search for the good life, the meaningful, satisfying life, is one of the oldest religious themes. From its earliest beginnings, religion has tried to connect people to God, to make a vast uncontrollable world seem less threatening. It has connected people to each other so that they would not have to celebrate or mourn alone. And as soon as human beings grew to understand that there was more to life than mere survival, they looked to religion to be their guide to the good life. In Judaism, in Christianity, and in several of the Oriental faith systems, religion is sometimes referred to as The Way, the path to living in harmony with the universe, the guide to living life as it was meant to be lived.

But we today have too often been disappointed when we tried to find guidance in the pages of our religious traditions. They say some very wise and true things, but there is a certainty to them which we often do not share. They speak so confidently of the existence of a God who controls the universe and reveals His will to us. They promise us happiness when we follow His ways and warn us of misfortune if we do not. We read that and we would like to believe it, but we find it hard. Experience so often seems to contradict that. The Bible and the books derived from it seem to be written for believers who can hear God's voice clearly and see His handiwork everywhere. They do not seem to be written for the troubled modern soul, for the skeptical, the doubting, the confused. The faithful are always saying, "Read the Bible, you will find answers there." But the restless, the seekers, the skeptics read it and find it a remote book, talking about things far from their concerns. The Bible's agenda does not seem to be their agenda, and its answers do not seem to fit their questions. Then they feel even worse to discover that something which has been so helpful to so many others does not seem to be speaking to them.

One book of the Bible, however, is unique, different from all the others around it. I would like to introduce you to the most unusual book in the entire Bible. If it were better known, it might be the most dangerous book in the Bible as well. Some people have thought of it that way. It is the Book of Ecclesiastes. Ecclesiastes is a small book, barely a dozen pages long in some editions, tucked all the way toward the end of the Hebrew Bible where many readers never get far enough to discover it. But the person who does find it and read it will be astonished by what it says. There is nothing quite like it in all of Scripture. It is the work of an angry, cynical, skeptical man who doubts God and questions the value of doing good. "What point is there in working hard?" he asks in the opening lines of his book. "A generation passes and another comes along, but the world remains the same forever." (Eccles. 1:4) "Man has no superiority over beasts, since both amount to nothing. As one dies, so does the other, and both have the same fate." (Eccles. 3:19) "In my own brief life I have seen this, that a good man perishes in spite of his goodness and a wicked man endures in spite of his wickedness, so do not exert yourself to be especially good, for you may be dumfounded." (Eccles. 7:15–16)

Does anyone else in the Bible talk like that? Virtually every other page of the Bible insists that our every deed, however small, matters. We are told that God cares about what we eat, whom we sleep with, how we make and spend money. Ecclesiastes comes and tells us that God does not in fact care about any of that. Rich people and poor, wise and foolish, righteous and wicked are all the same in His eyes. Irrespective of how they live, they all grow old and die and are soon forgotten. How they lived seems to make no difference.

There is a Jewish tradition telling us that when the sages met to fix the canon, to decide which ancient books would be part of the Bible and which ones would be left out, there was fierce debate over the Book of Ecclesiastes. Many found it offensive and threatening to their faith. They not only wanted to leave it out of the Bible, they wanted to ban it entirely, lest innocent young readers come upon it and be led into heresy by it. But somehow, even as they overcame their embarrassment at the eroticism of the Song of Songs and the *Arabian Nights* atmosphere of the Book of Esther, they made room for the cynicism and skepticism of Ecclesiastes.

What is this book that so upset the sages of old and so surprises the modern reader who chances upon it? It is a hard book to follow and understand. There is a unity of tone but no plot or story line and no constant development of a theme. The author jumps from subject to subject and sometimes contradicts himself, saying one thing and then its opposite on the same page. Some passages from the book will be familiar: "There is nothing new under the sun"; "To everything there is a season, a time to be born and a time to die"; "The sun also rises"; "Cast your bread upon the waters." But the book as a whole is not easily understood.

We do not know very much about the person who wrote the book. We do not even know his name or when in the thousand-year-long biblical period he lived. Because he describes himself as a descendant of King David and a ruler in Jerusalem, tradition attributes the book to King Solomon, the wisest man in the Bible. A Jewish tradition claims that Solomon is the author of three biblical books. When he was young and in love, he wrote the love poems in the Song of Songs. When he matured and turned his mind to making a living, he penned the practical wisdom of the Book of Proverbs. When he grew older, he gave voice to the feelings of cynicism and futility that we find in Ecclesiastes. Some scholars feel that it was this attribution to King Solomon that persuaded the ancient sages to overcome their doubts and include Ecclesiastes in the Bible.

Even his name, Ecclesiastes (in Hebrew, *Kohelet*), is obscure. As far as we know, no one else ever bore that name. Grammatically, it seems more like a title than a personal name (which should not be surprising; ancient authors almost never put their names on their work), and is usually understood to mean "the one who convenes an assembly, the one who calls people together." He may have been a teacher, a wise man who earned his living preparing the sons of the wealthy for the practical problems of living. Certainly his book, for all of its pessimism, has the tone of one who would share his experience with the young, not only instructing them but warning them.

Whether King Solomon actually wrote the book or not (the language seems to come from a much later period), it seems clear that the man we know as Ecclesiastes was a wise man in or past middle age, trying to deal with his fear of growing old and dying without ever feeling that he had really lived. He seems to be searching desperately for something to give his life enduring meaning.

I first discovered the book of Ecclesiastes when I was about seventeen, and I loved it at first sight. I loved the author's courage and honesty in attacking the orthodoxies of his time, pointing out the hypocrisy and exposing the shallowness of so much that passed for piety and wisdom in his day. I was fascinated with his wise observations on life, his cynical comments on human nature. They seemed so profound and pointed, so much more honest than the pious reassurances of most of the Bible. At the time, I thought that Ecclesiastes was like me, an idealistic young enemy of falsehood and foolishness, a challenger of pomp and pretense.

Now that I have reached the stage in life where Ecclesiastes probably was when he wrote his book, I realize how badly I misunderstood him when I was seventeen. I looked into the mirror of his book and saw my own image reflected back, an idealistic adolescent. But the author was not an adolescent. He was a bitter, weary man past the mid-point of his life. I caught the sharp point of his cynicism, deflating banality. I caught his delight in exposing the wishful thinking and outright falsehood that masquerade as religion. But because I was young when I first read the book, I completely missed the terror which, when I go back to read it now, is so obvious to me. This is a book by a very frightened man.

Ecclesiastes is not merely a wisdom teacher, more honest and forthright than most. He is not just an enemy of cant and hypocrisy. He is a man desperately afraid of dying before he has learned how to live. Nothing he has ever done, nothing he will ever do, makes any difference, he feels, because one day he will die and then it will be as if he had never lived. And he cannot handle that fear of dying and leaving no trace behind.

"The fate of the fool is destined for me as well; to what advantage then have I been wise? That too was futile because the wise man, like the fool, is not remembered. As the succeeding days roll by, both are forgotten. Alas the wise man dies just like the fool." (2:15–16)

In his book, he tells us the story of his life. He writes of his successes and his frustrations, of all the ways in which he tried to be successful and make something of his life, and of all the reasons why the question, What does it all mean in the long run? was never really answered. Ecclesiastes has been called the most personal book in the Bible. The prophets and other biblical authors sometimes tell us about their lives, their achievements and experiences. But no one else shares his innermost fears and frustrations with us the way Ecclesiastes does.

Ecclesiastes was apparently a man of many talents. In his youth, he set out to make money, and apparently did so. He writes, "I multiplied my possessions. I built myself houses and planted vineyards . . . I gained more wealth than anyone before me." (2:4,9)

But he learns that wealth is not the answer. He understands that he can lose his money as easily as he gained it. Or he can die, and someone else who never worked for it will inherit it. He has seen rich people spend their wealth foolishly, and he has seen them get sick and spend their last years in misery which all their wealth could not ease.

"There is an evil I have observed under the sun, and a grave one it is for man, that God sometimes grants a man riches, property and wealth, so that he does not want for anything, but God does not permit him to enjoy it. If a man beget a hundred children and live many years, but never find contentment, I would say that a stillborn child not even accorded a burial is more fortunate than he." (6:1-3)

Like many a rich young man, Ecclesiastes gives himself to pleasure, drinking and carousing and sampling all the other distractions that money can buy. "I said to myself, Come, I will treat you to merriment. I ventured to tempt my flesh with wine . . . I withheld from my eyes nothing they asked for . . . That too I found was futile. Of revelry, I said, what good is it?" (2:1,10,2) When he is young, he has no problems spending his time in pleasure. After all, like all young people, he has unlimited time, years stretching before him, and he can afford to squander some of them. But as he grows older and his time becomes more precious, he comes to understand that the life of uninterrupted fun is only a way of escaping from the challenge of doing something significant with his life. Having fun can be the spice of life but not its main course, because when it is over, nothing of lasting value remains.

Time, which was once the source of his advantage over older people, has now become his enemy. He is starting to realize that he is running out of time. Ecclesiastes has given us those memorable lines, "To everything there is a season, and a time to every purpose under heaven: a time to be born and a time to die, a time to plant and a time to uproot, a time to weep and a time to laugh, a time to mourn and a time to dance." (3:1-4) Now this middle-aged author is beginning to suspect that the good times are behind him, that most of the good things which will ever happen to him have already happened, and mostly it is the time of weeping and worrying that lies ahead. Joanne Greenberg has written a short story, "Things in Their Season," the title of which comes from Ecclesiastes. (It is found in her collection, *High Crimes and Misdemeanors,* Holt Rinehart & Winston, 1980.) In her story, a group of people inadvertently learn that the government is secretly taxing our time even as it taxes our income. (After all, time is money.) The more valuable your time is, the higher a bracket you are in. That is why busy people never seem to have enough time, no matter how efficient they are. The group hijacks a shipment of time from a government warehouse to extend the life of their beloved teacher, who is dying. But for Ecclesiastes, there is no way to steal time to extend his days.

Finding himself a man of leisure, his years of wild partying behind him, Ecclesiastes turns to learning in an effort to make sense of his life. Somewhere in all those books from the wisest men of the past, there must be the answer to his quest. By now, the reader senses a note of urgency in his searching. He is no longer asking, What does life mean? out of youthful intellectual curiosity. He is asking, What will *my* life mean? because he is beginning to sense the terrifying possibility that his life may be over soon and it will have meant nothing. Now when his searches lead him into blind alleys, he responds not with disappointment but with mounting despair. The most frustrating fact of all is the realization that death can come all too soon and wipe out all that life has labored for.

He sets out to test the popular proverb, "A wise man has eyes in his head, but the fool walks in darkness." (2:14) But what he learns is that if the wise man does in fact see more clearly, what he sees is the futility of life. The wiser he is, the more he sees unfairness, injustice, tragedy. He is now old enough that the shadow of death is beginning to creep into his consciousness and rob everything of meaning. What good is anything I do if it cannot protect me against dying and disappearing? What difference does it make if I am wise and my neighbor is foolish, if I am honest and he is wicked? In either event, the stories of our lives will end the same way. We will both die and be forgotten. All my learning, all my good deeds will die with me.

If wealth and pleasure did not give Ecclesiastes' life enduring meaning because they were so transitory, here today and gone tomorrow, what can we say about learning? The human mind is so fragile. Not only death but even old age, a stroke, senility can make all that learning disappear. Ecclesiastes may well have seen his own teachers grow old, their brilliance fading into cranky forgetfulness. To what purpose then should one exert oneself to be wise? The rich man loses his wealth when he dies, but the wise man may lose his wisdom even sooner.

There is one possibility remaining. One senses that Ecclesiastes hesitates to try this one, for fear that if it should fail there will be no hope left. He will have to conclude that life is in fact futile and meaningless. In his last desperate throw of the dice, an increasingly fearful Ecclesiastes turns to God. I will be pious, he says. I will follow all the teachings of my religion and look for that sense of peace and tranquility which has been promised to the pure of soul. Like many men and women his age, looking back on a life of struggle and conflict and looking ahead to an uncertain future, Ecclesiastes in middle age becomes religious. He finds time for those pursuits of the spirit for which he had been too busy or too sophisticated until now.

But they too fail him. He learns that even the highest level of piety cannot protect him from death and the fear of death, or from the oblivion to which death leads. No amount of righteous living can bring him to the point where he can bargain with God, where he can say to God, "Look at how valuable and admirable my life is. Isn't it in Your best interest that I should go on living rather than die and be forgotten?"

Is there no answer then? Is our need for meaning nothing more than wishful thinking, the grandiose arrogance of a species that is really no different from the "moth with no mouth"? Are we set on earth for one brief moment, to keep the species alive and then get out of the way of the next generation, so that it too will be able to reproduce and die? Has God planted within us a hunger which cannot be satisfied, a hunger for meaning and significance?

Ecclesiastes wrote his book many hundreds of years ago to share with us his disappointments and frustrations, to warn us that we should not waste our limited time as he did, in the illusion that wealth, wisdom, pleasure, or piety will make our lives matter. He tells us his story with mounting desperation, as one road after another leads to a dead end and he begins to see himself running out of years and running out of options. But he has not written his book only to express his frustration or to depress us. In the end, he has an answer. But it is an answer that makes sense only to someone who has shared his earlier dead ends and disappointments. That is why he offers it to us at the end of his story rather than at the beginning.

A Hasidic story tells of a man who went for a walk in the forest and got lost. He wandered around for hours trying to find his way back to town, trying one path after another, but none of them led out. Then abruptly he came across another hiker walking through the forest. He cried out, "Thank God for another human being. Can you show me the way back to town?" The other man replied, "No, I'm lost too. But we can help each other in this way. We can tell each other which paths we have already tried and been disappointed in. That will help us find the one that leads out."

Before we can begin to understand Ecclesiastes' conclusions, we have to accompany him on the false paths and dead ends he has written to warn us about. When we have learned, as he did so painfully and with so much frustration, which paths do not lead out, we will be better prepared to find and follow the one that does.

THREE

The Loneliness of Looking Out for Number One

IF you could live without limits, if you could do anything, go anywhere, command anyone to do what you wanted, would that make you happy? Would you be able to use all that power in ways that would give your life enduring significance and satisfaction?

One of the classics of world literature, Goethe's dramatic poem *Faust,* the story of the man who sells his soul to the devil, focuses on that question. Dr. Faust, the hero of the poem, is a middle-aged scholar and scientist who has just about given up hope that he will ever learn the true meaning of life. He has begun to fear that he will come to the end of his life honored and well educated but without ever having experienced what it means to be truly alive. That is why he makes his desperate bargain with the devil, promising the devil his soul in the hereafter in exchange for just one moment on earth so fulfilling that he will be moved to say, "Let this moment linger, it is so good."

The German poet Goethe spent his whole life writing his masterpiece *Faust.* He intended it to be his major statement about the meaning of life, the enduring literary masterpiece which would give his own life meaning. He began writing his play at the age of twenty, set it aside for other projects, then went back to it at forty (part of his own reaction to reaching mid-life, we may suspect), and completed it shortly before his death at age eighty-three. While we cannot be sure how old Goethe was when he wrote any particular line, it is fascinating to see how the hero's ideas of what he wants to do with his life change from the beginning of the story to its end.

At the outset of the play, the middle-aged Faust as pictured by a young Goethe wants to experience everything, to live without limits. He wants to read all the books, speak all the languages, taste all the pleasures. He wants to be like God, going beyond human limitations. So the devil gives him everything—wealth, political power, the ability to travel anywhere and be loved by any woman he desires. Faust does it all and he is still not happy. However much wealth he acquires, however many women he seduces, there is an unsatisfied hunger within him.

By the time we come to the end of the play, the author Goethe is in his eighties and his hero Faust has aged along with him. Instead of winning fights and attracting young women, Faust is now at work building dikes to reclaim land from the sea for people to live and work on. Instead of trying to be like God, a God of power, seeing and controlling without limits, he has now become like God, a God of creation, separating the water from the dry land, planting gardens and setting people to work in them. Now for the first time, Faust can say, "Let this moment linger, it is so good."

When we are young, we pursue success for its own sake. We want to find out how good we are. A man sells his home and moves to a different community, asking his wife and children to adjust to new friends and new schools, because a promotion at work requires it. A college athlete postpones graduate school to try out with a professional team. It may or may not make sense financially, but at that stage in our lives, it is hard for us to resist a challenge. It is not only the rewards of success that lure us on at that point; success itself is the reward. We want to find out how far our ability will carry us.

Then things change. Instead of seeing life as a contest and victory as an end in its own right, we start to see success as a means to an end. Instead of asking, How high can I climb? we start thinking in terms of, What sort of life will this make possible for me? The attractive young woman stops seeing the men in her life as a measure of how popular she is and starts asking herself what sort of husbands and fathers they might be, what sort of home she would have with them. The hard-driving businessman becomes less concerned with the next step up the corporate ladder and more concerned with translating his success into a life he can feel good about.

I can imagine that this is the path Ecclesiastes traveled. At first, he set out to make money because he was bright and ambitious, and that is what bright and ambitious people do. Though he never gives us the details, he apparently made a lot of money fairly easily and early in his life. "I built houses and planted vineyards for myself. I made myself gardens and parks, and planted in them all manner of fruit trees . . . I had male and female servants, and great herds and flocks, more than anyone else before me. I gathered for myself silver and gold, the treasures of kings and provinces." (2:4–8)

He seems to have everything going for him that a man

could possibly want. He seems to have no limits on his attainments. He is fabulously rich, impressively intelligent. Why then does he continue to feel that something is missing? Might it be that this sort of success somehow contains within itself the seeds of its own failure? Is there something about this striving for getting ahead which lets Act I of our lives be fulfilling and gratifying, but tends to make Act II inevitably disappointing?

To see the goal of life as "winning" forces us to see other people as competitors, threats to our happiness. For us to "win," they have to "lose." Their failure becomes one of the necessary ingredients of our success. In a competitive situation, whether it is a high school social setting or a baseball pennant race, there can be winners only if there are losers. Everyone who strives to be a winner finds that he has to set himself against the rest. He rises as they fall, and that outlook has its consequences.

Two true stories illustrate this. An American tourist found himself in India on the day of the pilgrimage to the top of a sacred mountain. Thousands of people would climb the steep path to the mountaintop. The tourist, who had been jogging and doing vigorous exercise and thought he was in good shape, decided to join in and share the experience. After twenty minutes, he was out of breath and could hardly climb another step, while women carrying babies, and frail old men with canes, moved easily past him. "I don't understand it," he said to an Indian companion. "How can those people do it when I can't?" His friend answered, "It is because you have the typical American habit of seeing everything as a test. You see the mountain as your enemy and you set out to defeat it. So, naturally, the mountain fights back and it is stronger than you are. We do not see the mountain as our enemy to be conquered. The purpose of our climb is to become one with the mountain and so it lifts us up and carries us along."

Second story: A friend of mine, a clergyman a few years older than I am, chose to share a very personal insight with me. He realized that something remarkable had happened to him about the time he grew too old to be called to a major pulpit. He discovered that he was no longer looking at his closest friends and colleagues in larger congregations and wondering when they would die or be caught in a scandal, thereby creating a promotional vacancy. He had never realized that he had been doing this, but his own concern for "moving up" and making something of his career had led him to see these fellow ministers as obstacles to his own happiness. His success could come only on the heels of their tragedy. For years, those feelings had made it hard for him to be genuinely friendly and open with colleagues and had made him dissatisfied with his own small congregation, despite its good points. He was turning himself into a lonely, jealous, bitter person. His sermons became harsh and judgmental, with little of the love or joy he claimed to represent, and he blamed others for his unhappiness. Now he finds that he has outgrown that sense of competitiveness. He can welcome colleagues as friends. He can serve as an unofficial mentor to younger ministers and accept his own congregants as being worthy of his love and care, rather than seeing them as symbols of his failure and lack of advancement. Nothing around him has changed but something inside him has changed, and he can look forward to his remaining years in the active ministry as being productive and gratifying ones.

Ecclesiastes worked to become wealthy and successful because for him wealth represented possibility, a life full of choices and comforts, knowing he would never have to do without something because he could not afford it. Faust yearned for wealth and success, because for him they were the key to power over other people. He believed that if he had enough money and influence, he could arrange things in his life to his satisfaction, and life would be good. There are two things wrong with that kind of thinking.

First, nobody can have that much power. The world is too complex and too elusive. You can never control everything that happens. Barbara Tuchman, in her book *The March of Folly,* examines the question of why leaders and nations behave foolishly in situations where it should be clear that what they are doing is hopelessly wrong. One of the recurring reasons for foolish behavior (the corruption of Roman emperors and medieval popes, Napoleon's and Hitler's invasions of Russia, America in Vietnam) is the notion that if you are powerful enough, you can impose your will on others and do whatever you want. One after another, they all learned that even overwhelming power is not enough to guarantee total control.

Second, the quest for wealth and power, and the exercise of that power, tends to separate you from other people. Not only does the quest for wealth lead many people to see life in terms of competition rather than cooperation, but the exercise of power by the successful can make human relationships difficult. If you love someone because he always tries to please you, because he does only what you want him to do, that is not love. That is just a roundabout way of loving yourself. Power, like water, flows downhill from someone in a higher position to someone lower down. Love can be generated only between people who see themselves as equals, between people who can be mutually fulfilling to each other. Where one commands and one obeys, there can be loyalty and gratitude but not love.

In the Bible, the sin of idolatry is not just a matter of bowing down to statues. Idol worship is treating the work of your own hands as if it were divine, worshipping *yourself* as the highest source of value and creativity. When the Second Commandment reads, "You shall not make yourself a graven image," one commentator takes that to mean not "You shall not make an idol *for* yourself," but "You shall not make an idol *of* yourself." Do not make *yourself* into an object of worship by believing that you have enough power to control the world in which you live and the other people who live in it.

Jean-Paul Sartre, the French philosopher and founder of the highly individualistic school of thought known as existentialism, once wrote, "Hell is other people." Sartre was a very wise man, but I think he said something very foolish on that occasion. Other people may complicate our lives, but life without them would be unbearably desolate. A leading anthropologist who had spent years studying chimpanzees in the wild once wrote, "One chimpanzee is no chimpanzee." That is, a chimpanzee can develop into a real chimpanzee only in the company of other chimps. Isolated in a zoo, it may survive but will never become its real self. I have been observing people in their natural habitat for at least as long as Dr. Leakey studied chimps, and I would paraphrase his comment to read, "One human being is no human being." None of us can be truly human in isolation. The qualities that make us human emerge only in the ways we relate to other people.

Hell is not "other people." Hell is having worked so hard for success that it corroded your relationships with other people, so that you learned to see them only in terms of what they could do for you. I think of Faust, having traded his soul for unlimited power in this world, and being so lonely in his unlimited power. For him, hell is the loneliness of having everything and knowing that it is still not enough. (Do we all make our bargains with the devil, gaining what we thought we wanted and losing part of our souls in the process?) I think of Ecclesiastes, surrounded by servants on his luxurious estate, perplexed by the question, If I have everything, why do I feel that something is missing? I think of Howard Hughes and Lyndon Johnson in their last years, experts at manipulating people to do their will, masters of the art of exercising power, ending up lonely old men surrounded by hired servants and favor seekers, wondering why so few people loved them.

Being in a position to exercise power over other people (employees, mates, children) may be gratifying for a little while, but never in the long run. Ultimately it leaves you lonely. You command, and you receive fear and obedience in return, and what emotionally healthy person can live on a diet of fear and obedience? Who wants people to be afraid of him, to obey him sullenly and grudgingly rather than freely and out of love?

Martin Buber, an important twentieth-century theologian, taught that our relationships with others take either of two forms. They are either I-It, treating the other person as an object, seeing him only in terms of what he does, or I-Thou, seeing the other as a subject, being aware of the other person's needs and feelings as well as one's own. Buber tells the story of an incident which changed his life and led him to that formulation. When he was young, his parents were divorced and he went to live with his grandparents on a farm. He would feed the animals, clean the pens, and groom the horses. One day, when Buber was about eleven, he was caring for a horse which was his particular favorite. He loved to ride and groom and feed that horse, and often brought it special treats, and the horse seemed to respond and like the boy who fed and combed it as well. As Buber was stroking the horse's neck, a strange feeling came over him. He felt that he could not only understand what it felt like to be an eleven-year-old boy patting a horse. Because he loved the horse, he could understand what it must have felt like to be a horse being patted by a boy. The joy of that moment, of being able to go beyond the confines of his own soul and know what another soul was experiencing, was so much more satisfying than the sense of power to make someone else do his will, that years later, Buber founded his entire theology on that feeling.

The Bible shows us two contrasting faces of God. Sometimes He is a commanding God, a God of Power, destroying Sodom, raining plagues on the Egyptians, splitting the Red Sea. And sometimes He is a helping God, a tender God, a God of Love and Relationship, visiting the sick, offering hope to the enslaved. We read those stories and we are understandably confused, because Love and Power are incompatible. You can love someone and give him the room and the right to be himself, or you can try to control him, to make him do your will whether for his own good or for the enhancement of your own ego. But you cannot do both at the same time. If you appreciate someone because he or she lets you do whatever you want and makes you feel strong and smart, that is not love. It does not recognize the uniqueness of the other person, only his or her usefulness. You could substitute anyone else who was equally compliant, and it would make no difference to you. Loving someone for being like you, for being an extension of your will, is not really love. It is just a round-about way of loving yourself.

Sometimes God's Power seems to get in the way of His Love. If we obey God because we are afraid of Him, because we don't want to offend Him, or because we are so overwhelmed by His might that we do not dare to challenge Him, then He has our obedience but He does not have our love. In order to love and be loved, God has to give us room to choose, to become ourselves. He cannot monopolize all the Power and leave none for us. The covenant between God and humanity has to be more than a matter of the Almighty laying down the Law. It has to be an agreement freely entered into between two free parties.

I think of all those passages in the prophecies of Hosea and Jeremiah which portray God as a husband whose wife has betrayed him, terribly audacious passages which almost picture God as lonely, longing for someone to love Him and not simply obey Him out of fear, grieving that His people do not love Him after all He has done for them. "I remember the devotion of your younger days, your love as a bride, how you followed Me into the wilderness, in a land not sown." (Jeremiah 2:2) "Have I been like a desert to Israel, a land of deep gloom? Why then do My people say, 'We have broken loose, we will not come to You any more'?" (Jeremiah 2:31) God is One, and because He is One, He is all alone unless and until there are people to love Him.

If we see ourselves as fashioned in the image of God, if we understand the image of God in us to represent what we will be like when we become full human beings, then which image of God shall we aspire to, the lonely God of Power or the loving God of Relationship?

I would like to believe that in the earliest stages of fashioning the Bible and the culture out of which it sprang, the Israelites pictured God in the image of the Near Eastern despots of the world they knew, Egyptian Pharaohs and kings of the Assyrian and Babylonian empires, absolute monarchs with the power to make or suspend laws, the power of life and death over their subjects. But then, I would like to think, their understanding of religion began to mature. They came to see that Power was not the absolute good, that the wielders of absolute power became not more than other humans but less than them, cruel and arbitrary, jealous and suspicious, inspiring fear but never love. And they could no longer picture God in that way. In the stories of Noah and the Flood or Abraham at Sodom, we already see God punishing people for being wicked to each other, not for not worshipping Him. The prophets speak of a God for Whom people being kind to each other is more important than bringing sacrifices to His altar. The image of a God of Power is never totally forgotten, but it is soon overshadowed by the image of a God who shares with us the task of building a humane world on the foundation of people caring for each other, even as He cares for each of us. God does not look out for number one; He looks out for the welfare of those least able to take care of themselves. In both the Law and the Prophets, in both the Hebrew Bible and the Christian New Testament, God has a special concern for the poor and the brokenhearted and a certain suspicion toward the rich and the successful not because it is good to be poor and immoral to be rich but because the poor and the afflicted seem to find it easier to need each other and to belong to each other. They tend to be more vulnerable, less self-satisfied, and there is something profoundly human about that.

We too must go through the same evolutionary process our ancestors went through, from worshipping power and success to idealizing helpfulness and caring relationships. My teacher Abraham Joshua Heschel used to say, "When I was young, I admired clever people. Now that I am old, I admire kind people."

There is nothing wrong with being successful. Churches, colleges, museums, and medical research all depend on the generosity of successful people sharing the fruits of their success with them. There is nothing wrong with having enough power to influence events. On the contrary, people who feel powerless and frustrated are more dangerous to society than people who know the effect of their influence and can use it wisely, because they may do desperate things to compel us to take them seriously. But there is something very wrong with the single-minded pursuit of wealth and power in a way which shuts us off from other people. It may put us in a position where the only thing worse than losing is winning.

There is a story behind the establishing of the Nobel Prizes, the supreme awards for achievement in the arts and sciences. Alfred Nobel, a Swedish chemist, made a fortune by inventing more powerful explosives and licensing the formula to governments to make weapons. One day, Nobel's brother died, and one newspaper by accident printed an obituary notice for Alfred instead. It identified him as the inventor of dynamite and the man who made a fortune by enabling armies to achieve new levels of mass destruction. Nobel had the unique opportunity to read his own obituary in his lifetime and to see what he would be remembered for. He was shocked to think that this was what his life would add up to, to be remembered as a merchant of death and destruction. He took his fortune and used it to establish the awards for accomplishments in various fields which would benefit humanity, and it is for that, not for his explosives, that he is remembered today. When Nobel was at his most "successful," he was working against life and against friendship. Then he realized what he would leave behind if that were all he did, and he gave the last part of his life another direction.

In recent years, a number of books have appeared on the theme of "looking out for number one." They suggest that it is a brutal, competitive world out there, and the only way to get ahead is ruthlessly to take advantage of other people's weaknesses. My objection to those books is not just that I disagree with their morality. I do, but why should anyone be impressed by that? (The philosopher Nietzsche once said that morality is a conspiracy of the sheep to persuade the wolves that it is wicked to be strong.) My objection to the "looking out for number one" philosophy is that it does not work. Take advantage of other people, use people, be suspicious of everyone, and you are liable to be so successful that you will end up far ahead of everyone else, looking down on them with scorn. And then where will you be? You will be all alone.

In the last few years, I have found myself traveling and lecturing a great deal. I have spoken in some thirty-eight states and six foreign countries. Often I am invited to the home of some prominent member of the community for dinner before my lecture, or for a reception afterward. Most of the time, my hosts are very gracious and the gatherings enjoyable. But every now and then I find myself uncomfortable in that setting, and one evening I finally realized why. Some people have to be very competitive to reach the top, and once they have gotten there, they find it hard to break the habit of competitiveness. They are not able to relax and chat with me. They feel that they have to impress me by telling me how successful they are, by dropping the names of important people they know. Sometimes they start an intellectual argument with me, trying to show me that they know more about my subject than I do. On those occasions, I find myself wondering why they feel they have to be so competitive, why they have to respond to a guest in their home as a competitor to be challenged, and whether part of the price they have paid for their success, part of their bargain with the devil if you will, is that they keep transforming friends into enemies.

I can understand why people who are now in their mid- to late thirties, the "baby boom" generation, might find a morality of self-interest attractive. For many of them, their early years were spent in institutions which were not ready for them, overcrowded double-session schools, new unfinished suburbs. Their college and young adult years were convulsed by the war in Vietnam. (A baby boy born in 1948, at the beginning of the baby boom, would have turned eighteen in 1966, when the draft calls were heaviest.) And while all young adults believe that their world is unprecedentedly different from the world of their parents, this generation may have had more reasons than most to think so. Technology, mobility, American power and affluence, the threat of nuclear war all made postwar American life drastically different from the world their parents had known in the Depression and war years. This new generation was given so many choices and so few guidelines for making them. They felt they were constantly being asked to pay for other people's miscalculations, sent to clean up other people's messes. No wonder they have grown up believing that people are out to get them, government is corrupt, authority is unreliable, businessmen are all crooks, and no one else has their best interests at heart even if they claim to. Their music, their movies, their mores all proclaim this distrust and disillusionment. Why shouldn't I look out for myself? That's what everybody else is doing.

Similarly, I can understand why a man (or occasionally but less often a woman) in his late forties will suddenly find a life of selfishness and self-indulgence irresistible, why he would leave his home in the suburbs for an apartment in a singles complex with pool and sauna, why he would swap his station wagon for a two-seater sports car, dye his hair and grow a beard (if it didn't come in too gray). He may be tired of a life of obligations, mortgage payments to meet, bills to pay, children to discipline. The humorist Sam Levenson used to say, "When I was a kid, they told me to do what my parents wanted. When I became a parent, they told me to do what my kids wanted. When do I get to do what I want?" I know a lot of middle-aged men who could say the same thing, but without laughing. They see this breakout not as a flight from responsibility and respectability, but as their last desperate chance to grab some joy and freedom in a life which will soon be two-thirds over and into its third and final act. (The story is told of a member of the Texas state legislature speaking in favor of a bill to outlaw certain kinds of sexual behavior who said, "There are three things wrong with this so-called New Morality. It violates the laws of God. It violates the laws of Texas. And I'm too old to take advantage of it.")

But even as I understand it, I can still see it as wrong. Not just morally wrong, something which offends God, but misguided, a policy that causes us to work hard but condemns us to end up somewhere other than where we wanted to be.

A man interviewed by Gail Sheehy for her book *Passages* (he has left his wife and is living with an eighteen-year-old girl he has just met) puts it this way: "The difficult thing for me to justify is leaving Nan [his ex-wife] high and dry because she hasn't done anything wrong. She's still in that other world where we were all brought up to live according to plans . . . What I've learned from the young people I've met out here is that there are no commitments." In other words, happiness is having no commitments, no one to answer to (which is the literal meaning of the word "irresponsible"), no one whose needs or problems will ever get in your way or tie you down.

The narcissists' creed, "I am not here to worry about your needs and I don't expect you to worry about mine. It's every man for himself," was not invented in the twentieth century. It is the latest formulation of an approach which is as old as mankind itself. It was Cain who said scornfully, "Am I my brother's keeper?" He said that not to justify his murder of his brother Abel but to justify his lack of concern for his brother's well-being: I look out for my best interests and he looks out for his. And what is Cain's punishment? He becomes a wanderer on the face of the earth, with no place to call home, with no community to support or comfort him. The original looking-out-for-number-one man, like all of his descendants, is condemned to spend all of his days unconnected.

In my all-time favorite movie, *Casablanca*, the hero Rick, played by Humphrey Bogart, is portrayed at first as a cynical, suspicious, self-protecting person. He stays ahead of the game by looking out only for himself and not giving in to tender feelings. When a desperate man is arrested by the Gestapo in Rick's bar, he asks Rick, "Why didn't you help me?" and Rick sneers, "I don't stick my neck out for anyone." Rick is living amid the cruelty and unfairness of the Second World War, and has learned that only the man who looks out for himself survives. He had been hurt by life when he made the "mistake" of taking someone else's welfare as seriously as he took his own. He has grown cynical, safe, and successful. But at some level, he realizes that something is missing from his life. Circumstances have forced him to become tough and uncaring, but he looks at the Nazi officers stationed in Casablanca, tough, powerful, unsentimental, and he knows that he does not want to be like them.

Flashes of decency break through during the movie, until at the end he gives up his chance for escape and happiness in an act of generosity to the woman he loves. She leaves for England; he is condemned to wander in North Africa. Like Faust, like the young Martin Buber, he found life unsatisfying when he worried only about himself. It was in the process of saving and enriching the lives of others that his own life began to take on meaning. Like Cain, Rick Blaine has become a man without a homeland. But unlike Cain, who condemned himself to exile by caring only about himself and refusing to be his brother's keeper, Rick feels himself alienated from life when he cares only about himself, and feels that he has come home to himself spiritually when he gives up home and wealth and security in an act of self-sacrifice. In some ways, he will now have less, but in ways he has come to consider more important, he has become whole.

FOUR

When It Hurts Too Much to Feel

I CAN imagine a world which is a mirror image of our world, identical but opposite, like the negative of a photograph or like a landscape reflected in a lake. What is high in our world is low in that other world; what is open here is closed there. There would be a sage in that world, a wise man like Ecclesiastes, but his opposite. He too would tell us the story of his frustrating quest for meaning in life's second act. But where our Ecclesiastes searched for the meaning of life in wealth, pleasure, and knowledge, his twin in the other world will have sought it in poverty, pain, and rejection of the intellect.

The Ecclesiastes of our world tried to make his life mean something by striving for wealth and power. He was disappointed because the quest for wealth and power isolated him from his fellow human beings, teaching him to see them as competitors and obstacles to success. Might one not be tempted to follow the exact opposite path, to base one's search for the meaningful life on learning to do without material things, on the renunciation of wealth and power?

Some people have in fact suggested that. Christian and

Buddhist monastic orders have asked their members to commit themselves to lives of voluntary poverty and humility, to escape the corruption and frustration that the quest for wealth entails. Almost a century ago, the great American philosopher and psychologist William James saw self-denial as a path to human happiness and self-fulfillment. He believed that wars were fought not so much for military reasons as for psychological ones, because in every generation men felt the need to test their courage and manhood. In his essay "The Moral Equivalent of War," James suggested that people could achieve the same goal less destructively by voluntarily practicing self-denial, getting into contests to see who could do without more creature comforts, who could endure more hardship than the next man.

Probably the greatest modern advocate of finding the true path of life by doing without worldly pleasures was Mahatma Gandhi, the spiritual father of modern India. When Gandhi became involved in his people's struggle for independence, he put aside the fancy clothes he had worn as a lawyer, wore a garment of plain white cloth, and lived and ate simply. (He once said that anyone who ate more than he needed to live was stealing food from someone else, and anyone who owned more clothing than he needed to cover himself was forcing someone else to do without.)

But in the century since William James wrote, there have been more wars and more people killed in wars than ever before. Demonstrating manly courage by doing without material comforts does not seem to have caught on as a substitute for fighting. Even the young people who dropped out of good colleges and family businesses in the 1960s to protest their parents' emphasis on material success have mostly found their way back to a modified "rat race." Mortgages and family responsibilities will do that to a person. The only remaining symbol of their rejection of their parents' comfortable lifestyle would seem to be a preference for stick shifts in their cars instead of automatic transmissions.

Monastic orders in the Western world are finding fewer people called to that life, and in India, few have chosen to follow the path of Gandhi. (And that may be just as well. To read Erik Erikson's psychological biography of Gandhi is to encounter the spiritual greatness of the man but at the same time to discover the sense of guilt and unworthiness which continually tormented him, causing him to afflict himself with hunger and other discomforts and to accuse people around him of terrible wishes which he must have found first in himself. Great people, I suppose, are entitled to quirks worthy of their stature, and we can admire Gandhi for his achievements and spiritual depths without having to accept his attitudes about food, sex, and comfort as a guide for our own personal quest.)

The Ecclesiastes of our world, finding himself free to do anything he wanted, pursued pleasure. Thousands of years later, Freud would suggest that the search for pleasure was indeed the guiding principle of a healthy person's life. He taught that much human behavior, like the behavior of other living creatures, is determined by the effort to maximize pleasure and minimize pain. We act differently from animals only because our understanding of what is pleasurable and what is painful differs from theirs. So Ecclesiastes lost himself in wine, women, and entertainment, until he realized how empty and futile such a life was. Fun can be the dessert of our lives but never its main course. It can be a very welcome change of pace from the things we do every day, but should it ever become *what* we do every day, we will find it too frivolous a base to build a life on.

I think of all the people I knew (and envied) in high school whose lives seemed to be so much more full of fun than mine—the athletes, the good-looking, smooth-talking students, the first ones to have serious boyfriends or girlfriends. We all envied them back then, because their lives seemed to be one long party, one fun experience after another. Neither they nor we could have known back then that a life of constant pleasure during those teenage years almost inevitably sets one up for a life of frustration afterward. There are skills not acquired, habits not formed, and lessons about the real world not learned during those years of having everything go smoothly for you.

Have you ever noticed how an illness early in life, if not too severe, can teach a person to take sensible care of his health ever after? Or how growing up with financial limitations gives one a realistic notion of what it means to earn or spend a dollar? Or how the frustrations of adolescence can teach a person compassion and sensitivity? In the spirit of Jung's observation that "only the wounded doctor can heal," how can a young person to whom things have always come easily learn the lessons of patience, hard work, and tolerance for failure in others? Perhaps that is why the most naturally talented ball players often turn out to be poor coaches. They don't know how to teach others to achieve what came so effortlessly to them. Will someone to whom things came effortlessly in youth ever learn the disciplines of patience and postponing gratification, or will that person be unprepared for the day when the music stops and people start saying no?

How sad to have your high school years be the high

point of your life, and have everything run downhill from there. Irwin Shaw has written a short story called "The Eighty-Yard Run," which I read many years ago and have never forgotten. A college freshman, at his first football practice, breaks loose for an eighty-yard touchdown run. His teammates look at him with awe. His coach says, "You're going to have quite a future around here." His blond girlfriend picks him up after practice and kisses him warmly. He has the feeling that life is completely satisfying. But nothing in the rest of his life ever lives up to that day again. His football experiences never rise above the level of mediocrity. His business career is equally disappointing, his marriage sours, and the pain of failure is even greater because he remembers thinking on a perfect day many years before that life would always be that pleasant.

I think of a woman in my congregation who, some years ago, found her way out of a disastrous marriage. She was young, attractive, had a good job, and was so emotionally scarred that she was in no hurry to enter into a new relationship. For some years, she has been part of the "swinging singles" scene. Today she looks at me over her third cup of morning coffee and an ashtray full of cigarette butts, and says, "I know people envy me—the parties, the vacations, the freedom from responsibility. I wish I could make them understand how much I envy them. I wish I could tell them how soon it all gets to be dull and repetitious, until you find yourself doing things you really don't want to do, just not to be doing the same thing all over again, and how quickly I would trade all of this for the sound of a car door closing and familiar steps coming up the stairs at night."

If Ecclesiastes' pursuit of pleasure was unsatisfying, like a snowflake that looks so beautiful as it floats to earth but disappears the instant you try to take hold of it, what path might the sage of our imaginary mirror-image universe pursue? Is there a way in which he might try to find his life's meaning in the deliberate taking on of pain? It sounds strange, but some people do just that. Their cry, like Faust's, is, "I want to know that I have lived," and the answer that comes back to them is, "The only worthwhile life is the life of suffering and self-sacrifice. Living for yourself never brings satisfaction. Only living for others does."

I have known people who chose to play the role of martyr (or arranged to have that role assigned to them) in a family or work setting, taking all the pain and all the blame on themselves. They seemed to have no wishes of their own except to carry out other people's wishes. They seemed comfortable only when they were being exploited or taken advantage of by others. Some were wives of alcoholics, drug addicts, or compulsive gamblers. Some were men or women whose spouses abused them physically or psychologically, beating them with fists or words. (I remember once calling on a woman in the congregation who had told me that she needed to discuss her marital problems. She offered me what was probably the worst cup of coffee I have ever tasted, a spoonful of instant coffee mixed with warm tap water, and proceeded to tell me of her conflicts with her husband while I pretended to sip it. "He's always putting me down. Nothing I ever do is any good in his eyes. He's constantly criticizing me. I can't stand it anymore. I think if I hear another word of criticism, I'll kill myself. How is your coffee, Rabbi? Would you like another cup?")

These people seem characterized by an almost total lack of self-worth. They seem to feel that they have no right to do anything for their own sakes, but only to submerge themselves in meeting the needs of others. Perhaps early in life, someone taught them—their parents, or even their religious teachers—that they were no good, and they have come to feel that the only way they can justify their existence is by becoming a doormat for others. They seem unhappy about the pain in their lives, but at the same time they seem resigned to it and reluctant to do anything to change it. They seem to believe that they deserve to suffer.

Too often, the voice of religion has been heard to justify suffering, to tell people that it is their "cross to bear," the fate that God has wished for them or the fate that they have brought down on themselves by their sinful thoughts and deeds. People have been told to love their afflictions, and they do their best to do that.

These are relatively rare and extreme cases, of course, but they are the extreme form of a much more common phenomenon, the attitude of the person who says to himself, "It's not right for me to be this comfortable. I don't deserve it. I have to do something to myself to balance it off." What we are dealing with is one of the fundamental conflicts in the American character. On the one hand, we are a terribly self-indulgent people. We squander so much of the world's energy resources to keep ourselves warmer in winter and cooler in summer than most people find necessary. We equip our cars more lavishly than people in other countries furnish their homes, with plush seats, air conditioning, and stereophonic music. We like to eat well, dress well, live well. But at the same time, we are the spiritual children of the Puritans who settled these shores, and that heritage makes us feel guilty when we have enjoyed too much physical comfort. People were not meant to live so well, a voice whispers inside us, and we had better atone for that.

To the Puritans, life was a grim, serious business, and sin was always lurking to tempt us from the proper path. They actually passed laws against laughing on Sunday, the Lord's Day. Their idea of entertainment was sitting on a hard wooden bench in church listening to a three-hour sermon on the torments of hell. (Someone once defined a Puritan as a person who would abolish bullfighting not because it caused the bull pain but because it gave the spectators pleasure.)

We Americans have inherited these two tendencies, and have never learned how to reconcile them and live comfortably with both. We are constantly getting into cycles of indulging ourselves, feeling guilty, and punishing our bodies to make up for it. We overeat and then we diet; we drive two blocks to the mailbox, and then drive a mile farther to the gym or swimming pool to work out. It is as if we felt some inner compulsion to punish ourselves for the "sin" of feeling comfortable.

Why does Lorraine, who has been married for less than a year to a man she loves very much, have so much trouble relaxing and enjoying making love with her husband? Why does she keep remembering her mother's scoldings and warnings when she would leave on a date or come home from one? Why can't she get over feeling guilty whenever she experiences something pleasant?

Why does Harry, a forty-four-year-old businessman, leave the swimming pool of his Florida hotel to call his office twice a day? Why does he feel he is being irresponsible and self-indulgent if he tries to relax and enjoy his vacation, and why does his wife always complain about the food at their luxury hotel? Why does Max, who was born in Europe, brought to this country as a child, and is now a successful entrepreneur, give so generously to any charity which features a picture of a hungry child? Do we all hear voices telling us that we don't deserve our good fortune? Do we all secretly believe that there is something bad about feeling good, that anything enjoyable can't possibly last because we don't deserve it?

I think there *is* a sense in which many people seek out pain to "balance" the comforts and pleasures of their lives. I remember when I was jogging. Until I strained my knee a few years ago, I would be out there running my three to five miles every other morning, wearing my T-shirt with ISAIAH 40:31 printed on the back. (The verse reads, "Those who trust in the Lord will have their strength renewed. They shall mount up with wings as eagles. They shall run and not grow weary." It didn't help.) I would look at the other runners on the streets near my home, their bodies glistening with sweat, their eyes gazing intently ahead, seeing that same look of determination on their faces that they undoubtedly saw on mine. Our running had none of the spontaneous exuberance of a child at play or the easy grace of a natural athlete. There was a sense of grim, dogged commitment to it, almost an air of religious penance. I can remember how I would urge my protesting body on for another mile by saying to myself, "I have sinned by being too indulgent with my body. I have driven when I might have walked. I have eaten and drunk too much, reaching for that extra piece of pie when I should have known better. I have sat at my desk too long. Therefore I must atone for that by punishing myself, afflicting my body with jogging, submitting it to the Nautilus machines, until I hurt so much that I feel satisfied that my body has paid the price for its self-indulgence." (Notice the separation in my thinking between the body that sinned and must suffer, and the spirit which judges and punishes it.) So gymnasiums across the country are hung with signs reading "No pain, no gain" and "If it doesn't hurt, you're not doing it right." We seem to contradict Freud by welcoming pain and actually taking pleasure in it.

The conflict may go even deeper than that. It may represent one of the fundamental splits in the soul of Western civilization. Our civilization is drawn basically from two roots, the Greek and the Judeo-Christian. The Greeks, like all peoples before the rise of biblical Judaism and the emergence of Christianity, were pagans. Paganism was more than simply worshipping many gods. It was a deification of nature, treating whatever was natural as divine. For the pagans, God was manifested in the rain, the harvest, the cycles of the sun and the seasons, and in the form and fertility of human bodies. At the most crude level, the pagan gods and goddesses were rainmaking and fertility charms. Imagining a parallel between the rain making the field fertile and the male semen making women fertile, pagan people would have wild sexual orgies in the spring to encourage the growth of the crops and the birth of many babies. They would have more orgies in the fall to express gratitude for the harvest, and sometimes orgies at the time of the winter solstice to strengthen the fading winter sun. (I guess that when it comes to having orgies, any excuse will do.) The Bible describes with disgust the cult prostitution in the Temples of Baal, the Canaanite rain god.

In its more sophisticated form, as in ancient Greece, paganism expressed itself in the worship of beauty and symmetry. It gave us the architecture of the Parthenon, the stunning statues of the male and female bodies, and the worldview captured many centuries later in Keats's "Ode on a Grecian Urn":

> *Beauty is truth, truth beauty,—that is all*
> *Ye know on earth, and all ye need to know.*

But beauty is not necessarily truth. A beautiful person can be vain, selfish, disloyal. A beautiful building may be the site of corruption and dishonesty. The Bible rejected the ideas that nature was divine and beauty was truth, and insisted instead that righteousness was truth. The Book of Proverbs warns us that "grace is deceitful and beauty is vain, but the woman who fears the Lord shall be praised."(31:30) Nature is not divine. It is part of God's creation and, like the rest of God's handiwork, can be used for good or misused for evil.

The biblical rejection of paganism may go back as far as the scene in the Garden of Eden when Eve sees the forbidden fruit as being "good for eating and a delight to the eyes," and follows her appetite rather than her sense of right and wrong. If I had to summarize the moral thrust of the Bible in one sentence, it would be, "Don't do what you feel like doing; do what the Lord asks of you." Biblical sexual morality, the dietary laws of the Hebrews, the emphasis on charity to the poor and justice for the foreigner were all efforts to teach people to override their "natural impulses." To this day, Jews abstain from food, drink, and sex on Yom Kippur, the Day of Atonement, not in order to punish themselves for their sins and cause God to feel pity for them, but in order to symbolize dramatically the human ability, which no other animal has, of controlling our instincts. Animals will reject spoiled food; they can be restrained physically or by fear of punishment from eating or mating. But they cannot abstain voluntarily. Only human beings (and I sometimes think not all human beings) can do that. Where the pagans saw divinity in the fulfilling of man's natural instincts (that modern spokesman for paganism, Ernest Hemingway, once defined "moral [as] what you feel good after and what is immoral is what you feel bad after"), the Bible found the image of God in the human ability to control instinct.

The paganism with which the Hebrew Bible took issue was the crude, blatantly sexual paganism of Canaanite farmers concerned mainly with making war, growing crops, and making babies. But in the centuries between the two Testaments, Israel was conquered by Alexander the Great, and the people encountered paganism in its more sophisticated Greek version. Greek culture was not fertility rites and Baal worship. It was the philosophy of Plato and Aristotle, the drama of Aeschylus and Sophocles. It was architecture, art, and sculpture. Still, from the biblical point of view, Greek culture was fatally flawed because it continued to regard beauty and pleasure as divine, rather than as two of God's minor creations. The Greeks, for their part, could never understand the Jewish lack of regard for physical beauty. Why didn't they exercise more? Why didn't they display their bodies for people to admire? Why did they feel they were obeying God when they defaced the perfection of His creation by circumcising their sons?

In James Michener's novel *The Source,* there is a classic confrontation scene between Jew and Greek, set in the year 168 B.C., just before the revolt of the Maccabees. Jehubabel, leader of the Jewish community, has an appointment with the local Greek governor Tarphon, to bring a complaint about one of the Emperor's new laws. They meet at the gymnasium, where Tarphon has been exercising. The governor is completely naked, exulting in the exercise of his body in the sunlight. The Jewish representative, in contrast, is so completely dressed that only his eyes and nose are exposed. Neither one is able to understand why the other is dressed (or undressed) as he is. Each sees the other's manners as a form of blasphemy.

By the time of the New Testament, the land of Israel was part of the Roman Empire, which combined Greek culture with Roman military and political skill. The religious leaders of early Christianity were so repelled by the flagrant sensuality of Roman life—its nudity, its homosexuality, its excessive eating and drinking—that they found themselves condemning almost all bodily pleasures as inherently sinful. They taught a distinction between the soul, which was pure, holy, and nonphysical, and the body, which was gross, subject to decay, and the cause of sin. For whatever reason, perhaps to test it, the soul found itself trapped in a body of clay during its stay on earth. But God wanted it to resist the temptations of the flesh and return to Him pure and unsullied. Voices in early Christianity responded to the excesses of Roman life—the casual sex, the ostentatious displays of wealth, the gluttony —with extremism of their own, becoming mistrustful of any sexual contact, any wealth, any wine or rich food.

In the early Middle Ages, when violence, lust, and the pursuit of wealth dominated European society and even infected the highest levels of the Church, the most sensitive religious souls turned their backs on the world and founded monastic orders based on the ideals of poverty and chastity. Again there seemed to be no middle ground.

One either lost oneself in a world of material goods and sensual pleasure, or else fled from that world and all of its sinful temptations, and taught one's soul to dominate one's body.

We are all children of the modern Western world, shaped by the influence of the Bible, the Church, and Greek culture. We have inherited both the Greek love of physical pleasure and the biblical ambivalence about it. We are torn between finding physical pleasures irresistible and finding them shameful and guilt-producing. We have never really made up our minds about sex, sometimes seeing it as the master key to happiness, sometimes seeing it as the cause of most of the world's misery and perversion. We tell jokes about sex because the subject makes us anxious, and humor is one of the ways we deal with our anxiety. "Vice squads" and "morals charges" deal almost exclusively with sexual matters, as if there were no other ways of being vicious or immoral except sexual ones. We watch movies and buy magazines glorifying the nude or nearly nude human body, but we still feel vaguely guilty and uncomfortable as we do so—some of us uncomfortable with that much sexual freedom, some of us rejecting the exploitation of that which should be revered privately —because spiritually we are children of both Athens and Jerusalem.

We have never really made up our minds about food. Clearly it means more to us than simply nourishment, fuel for our bodies. Food becomes a symbol of love; starting when we were only hours old, someone showed us that she loved us by giving us something to eat. Food represents reward and reassurance. When we are hurt, angry, lonely, afraid, we calm ourselves with food. But food also represents temptation (remember Eve?), the proof that we are weak-willed, self-indulgent creatures who deserve to be condemned for our weakness.

When the pagan half of our souls has control over us, we indulge our appetites too much, too richly, too often. When the Puritan side takes over, we punish ourselves. (Interestingly, the words "pain" and "punish" come from the same Latin root.) We diet, we exercise beyond the point of pleasure, or we reject the idea that eating should be a pleasant experience at all. It becomes an inconvenient, unpleasant necessity, like some people's view of sex. We come to tolerate bread that tastes like cotton and vegetables indistinguishable in taste from the plastic they come wrapped in, because caring too much about how food tastes is a form of weakness and gluttony. We invent fast foods and drive-through restaurants so that we hardly have to eat at all.

It should be eminently clear that we cannot possibly be content if we are constantly at war with ourselves, if our bodies and our consciences are engaged in perpetual struggle, one calling the other a pervert and the other responding by shouting back, "Prude!" We ask, How shall I live? and one of the voices inside our heads shouts, "Enjoy yourself!" while another urges us, "Abstain!" We want to have fun but we keep telling ourselves, This is frivolous; why am I doing this? We try to affirm the seriousness of life, only to find ourselves asking, Who am I kidding? Ecclesiastes, who may have been the first biblical author to be both a Jew and a Greek, also heard those two voices, one saying to him, "Life is short. Don't squander it; enjoy it while you can, for who knows how long you will be around?" while the other kept saying, "Life is short; don't waste it on this here-today-gone-tomorrow vanity." No wonder he was confused.

Whether this inner conflict stems from our mixed Greek–Judeo-Christian heritage or (as with Gandhi) from the Eastern ambivalence about the body and material things in general, we will never know rest until we find a way out of the cycle of indulgence and guilt and self-denial, sex and shame, binge and diet. How can we even approach inner peace and contentment when one half of us hates and scorns our other half?

Let me share with you what I think is one of the most profound religious thoughts I know. In the Talmud, the collected wisdom of the rabbis of the first five centuries, it is written, "In the world to come, each of us will be called to account for all the good things God put on earth which we refused to enjoy." Isn't that a remarkable statement for a religious leader to make? No scorn, no disgust for the body and its appetites. Instead, a sense of reverence for the pleasures of life which God put here for our enjoyment, a way of seeing God in the world through the experience of pleasant moments. Like all gifts, of course, they can be misused, but then the fault is ours, not God's. We have all seen people throw themselves into eating or drinking or sex or spending money, to such a degree that they no longer enjoy doing these things. The compulsive drinker, the compulsive philanderer soon gets to the point where he can't even enjoy his whiskey or his sexual affairs. He keeps reaching for them only to still the pain, to make the need go away. But used properly, all of these appetites come to be seen as God's gifts to us, to add pleasure to our lives. (I recently discovered a similar attitude in a Roman Catholic convent which would accept a candidate for holy orders only if she "ate well, slept well, and laughed easily.")

To view the human body and the whole natural world

with disgust or mistrust is as much a heresy as to view it with unqualified reverence. The person who seeks out pain and discomfort because she has come to believe that she deserves it, that it is sinful to find life easy and pleasant, is as misled as the person who mindlessly seeks out pleasure as the sole purpose of being alive. Both alike will come to Ecclesiastes' melancholy conclusion, "What have I gained from all this? This too is futile."

FIVE

Feeling No Pain,
Feeling No Joy

A BOUT a year after my book on coping with suffering came out, I was invited to take part in a conference at Randolph-Macon College in Ashland, Virginia, entitled "Five Religious Perspectives on Suffering." It was one of the most stimulating weekends I have ever spent. I was the Jewish representative, along with a Christian, a Buddhist, a Moslem, and a Hindu, each of us explaining his or her faith's perspective on why people suffer and what religion can tell them to do about it.

The Hindu representative explained to me over dinner one night that his religion taught him to deal with pain and suffering not by denying it or ignoring it but by rising above it. His religion taught him to say to the most painful experiences imaginable, "I will not let you hurt me. I will experience the worst that can happen and triumph over it. I will learn the art of detachment and transcend the pain." We have all seen pictures of Hindus walking on hot coals or resting on beds of sharp nails. They are doing with their bodies what they try to do with their souls, teaching themselves not to feel the pain. The pain is real, but it does not hurt. I remember reading of how G. Gordon Liddy of

Watergate fame would show how tough he was by holding his hand over a burning flame. When asked, "Doesn't that hurt?" he would answer, "Of course it hurts. The trick is not to let yourself feel it."

My dinner companion said to me that evening, "How lucky you are to have lost a child when you were so young, so that you could learn to conquer grief and pain. Most people don't have an opportunity like that until they are much older." He went on: "When a person dies, it is not a tragedy. His soul returns to the great stream of Life, like a drop of water returning to the ocean, its source. Dying is not painful. It is living that is painful, because being alive isolates us from the rest of life and leaves us vulnerable. When we complete our period of individual existence, we rejoin the stream of Life. Your son's life was pain-filled and tragic, and not only because he was sick. Everyone's life is pain-filled and tragic. But his death was not tragic. His death brought him peace, and it should have brought you peace and a sense of completeness as well, except that your habit of wanting things, wanting health, wanting children, wanting everything to turn out favorably, keeps you in pain." He leaned across the table and said to me, "You are a wise man and a fine writer but you still have to learn the most important truth of all: Nobody suffers in this world except people who want things they cannot have. When you learn not to desire, you will rise beyond suffering."

I looked at him incredulously. Here was a man I liked personally and respected for his religious sincerity. But what he was saying was so totally the opposite of what I felt and believed. What his religion taught him about life and death was so different from what mine taught me. I did not feel lucky to have lost a son whom I loved. Neither had I achieved tranquility or transcended the pain. (To that, my friend would have replied that my mourning and religious growth were still incomplete.) The sense of loss still hurt years later, though I had learned to live with it. More than that, I believed that *it was supposed to hurt.* In the same way that dead cells, our hair and fingernails, feel no pain when they are cut but living cells bleed and hurt, so I believe that spiritually dead souls can be cut into, separated from other souls, and not feel pain. But living, sensitive souls are easily hurt.

I don't like being hurt. I don't enjoy experiencing pain. But I believe that I become less of a human being if I learn the art of detachment so well that I can experience the death of a friend or relative, or watch a television news show about starving children, and not be emotionally affected by it. Maybe people living in a land of grinding poverty, infant mortality, and frequent floods, famines, and natural disasters have to armor themselves against the constant threat of calamity, the way doctors have to protect themselves against becoming too emotionally close to the seriously ill patients they treat. But I feel that the price we pay for that sort of protection is too high.

When I protect myself against the danger of loss (by death, divorce, or just having a close friend move away) by teaching myself not to care, not to let anyone get too close to me, I lose part of my soul. When I try to avoid pain by skipping the articles about famine and torture in the papers and turning to the sports pages and gossip columns, saying to myself, "It's too bad but that's the way the world is," I let myself become less human, less alive. When I protect myself from disappointment by not wanting to be happy, by telling myself that happiness is a mirage and an illusion, I diminish my soul. To be alive is to feel pain, and to hide from pain is to make yourself less alive.

My Hindu friend at the weekend conference was talking about transcending pain and sorrow, accepting them and absorbing them rather than fighting them. (Oriental religion in general tends to see things in terms of the blending of opposites to produce a sense of the whole. Where Western religion tends to see sharp contrasts between, for example, male and female, divine and human, good and evil, for the Eastern believer the dividing lines are much less clear.) He was not talking about denying pain and hiding from it, the way many people do. Too often, if something hurts us, either we pretend it does not hurt, or we take a pill to make the pain go away, without ever dealing with the real cause of the pain. Maybe we are supposed to hurt, and hiding from the pain only enables us to evade that lesson. Nobody ever tells us that there are dangerous side effects to the habit of turning to painkilling medications, and one of them is our diminished ability to feel anything at all.

So often, I officiate at a funeral and the bereaved relatives in the front row are manifestly uncomfortable. They know they ought to be feeling something—grief, pain— but they do not feel anything because they have never learned how to let themselves feel. Except perhaps for anger and annoyance, they have never learned the language of emotions, and now that they need to express themselves in it, they find themselves tongue-tied. So often, when I am alone with the family in the moments before the funeral service, there will be an old woman crying at the top of her voice, "Why? Why did this have to happen? He was so good!" And there will be a forty-year-old man in a three-piece suit who will become very uncomfortable and say, "Can't somebody make her shut up? Can't somebody give her a sedative?" The fact is, the old woman is the only one in the room who is in her right mind. She knows that something painful has happened to her, and she is responding to it. The rest of us are too numb, too inarticulate in the language of grief, to know what is happening to us.

My dinner companion was telling me that the way to get through a life full of tragedy and uncertainty was to accept it and yield to it, rather than fight it, like an Oriental wrestler using his opponent's weight and strength against him rather than trying to meet him head-on. But he also tried to tell me that the way to keep from going through life in constant pain was to lower your expectations. Do not expect life to be fair, and you will not have your heart broken by injustice. There have always been crime, corruption, and accidents, and there always will be. It is part of the human condition. (A teacher of mine used to say, "Expecting the world to treat you fairly because you are a good person is like expecting the bull not to charge you because you are a vegetarian.") Ecclesiastes let himself in for so much pain and confusion because he let the imperfection of the world get to him. There was no need for him to be so upset by it. His life would have been so much more pleasant had he learned to shrug his shoulders at suffering and unfairness, and say, "I am truly sorry that this is the way the world is, but I won't change it by being aggravated by it, so why be aggravated?"

Do not let anything become that important to you—not your job, not your car, not even your health or your family —and you will make yourself immune to the fear of losing them. Instead of working so hard to raise the level of what you have to equal what you want (or what advertisers have persuaded you to want), lower the level of what you want to that which you already have, or even lower, to the level of what cannot ever be taken away from you. Then instead of frustration and want, you will have tranquility and peace of mind.

In the Second World War, the Nazis rounded up innocent civilians by the millions and sent them to concentration camps. Those prisoners whose sense of self depended on their wealth, their social position, their prestigious jobs tended to fall apart when those things were taken away from them. The prisoners whose sense of self grew out of their religious faith or their own self-esteem, rather than other people's opinion of them, tended to fare much better.

The Talmud makes a similar point when it says, "Who is wealthy? He who is content with what he has." Measure a man's wealth not by how much he has, but by how much he wants and does not have. A rich man who, because of some psychological hunger, feels he needs still more is not really rich.

I listened respectfully to what my dinner companion was telling me that evening, and was moved and enlightened by much of it. But ultimately I had to disagree. When it was my turn to speak and his turn to eat his meal, I suggested that when we lower our expectations of life to avoid the pain of disappointment, we forfeit part of the image of God in us. To accept crime and political corruption because they have always been part of society is to give up too easily. Yes, it will spare us much anguish and frustration, but at what cost? To become less attached to my children, less ambitious about my work because life is unfair and unpredictable immunizes me against great pain but also serves to rob me of great hope and great joy. Like the man at the funeral who wishes the best but advises badly when he says, "Can't someone give her a sedative?", like the overprotective father who won't let his child ride her bicycle for fear she will fall and hurt herself, we envelop ourselves and each other with misdirected concern. Putting on the armor keeps us from being hurt, but it also keeps us from growing.

And yet we have to grow. Any woman who has had a baby knows how much pain is involved in giving birth to a new life. In a sense, it is almost as painful to give birth to a new self during our lives, to outgrow the person we used to be, shed the skin which protected us so well, and take on the risk of a new identity. Being an adolescent was a painful experience for many of us, because we were giving birth to a new self, a new sense of who we were. And changing our habits later in life can be an equally painful, and equally necessary, ordeal.

I am the rabbi of a congregation of some six hundred families, many of them young parents in their thirties and forties. I have seen the impact of the epidemic of divorce and marital conflict on the families of my congregation, sometimes affecting as many as one-third of the members of a given age bracket. I have seen what divorce does to adults and to children.

Adults hurt, but for the most part they survive intact. If forty percent of marriages end in divorce, eighty percent of divorces end in remarriage, often very stable and satisfying remarriages. And even when both parties may not remarry, they often experience a degree of personal growth, once the initial hurting is over. I have had any number of women tell me that going through a marital separation, with its financial worries and sense of rejection, was painful, but once they came to terms with what had happened, they found themselves stronger, happier, and more independent than they had ever been before. Many of them found, through necessity, that they were capable of being much more resourceful and competent than they ever knew they could be. Instead of being one half of a married couple, they found themselves being whole people in their own right.

But young children are often more vulnerable, less able to take charge of their own lives and put things back together. Some of the effects of divorce on children are all too familiar to us: the sense of rejection, the guilt that they may have caused the split, the absence of a role model. But from what I have seen, the most damaging effect of divorce on children, and even on their friends who have not experienced a divorce personally but have heard so much about it, goes beyond these. I am afraid that we may be raising a generation of young people who will grow up afraid to love, afraid to give themselves completely to another person, because they will have seen how much it hurts to take the risk of loving and have it not work out. I am afraid that they will grow up looking for intimacy without risk, for pleasure without significant emotional investment. They will be so fearful of the pain of disappointment that they will forgo the possibilities of love and joy.

So Simon and Garfunkel sang to the young people of the sixties, "If I never loved, I never would have cried . . . I touch no one and no one touches me . . . I am a rock, I am an island . . . and a rock feels no pain, and an island never cries." Psychologist Herbert Hendin has written of the fear of true intimacy in people growing up today. Serious involvement is a trap; it limits your options. Caring leaves you vulnerable to disappointment and rejection.

Having children does not represent fulfillment and immortality, but obligation and inconvenience. He writes: "Twenty years ago, detachment and inability to feel pleasure were considered signs of schizophrenia. Today, people believe that emotional involvement invites disaster, and detachment offers the best means of survival." In our work, in our play, even in our sexual lives, we want to be like machines (we speak of being "turned on"), performing but not caring too deeply.

A young couple came to see me one evening in my study. I would be officiating at their wedding in a few months, and because I did not really know them, I asked them to come in so that we could meet each other and go over the marriage ceremony. At one point, the young man said to me, "Rabbi, would you object to one small change in the wedding ceremony? Instead of pronouncing us husband and wife till death do us part, could you pronounce us husband and wife for as long as our love lasts? We've talked about this and we both feel that, should the day come when we don't love each other anymore, it's not morally right for us to be stuck with each other."

I said to them, "Yes, I do object, and no, I'm not going to make that change. You and I both know that there is such a thing as divorce, and you and I both know that a lot of marriages these days don't last until one of the partners dies. But let me tell you something. If you go into this marriage with an attitude of 'If it doesn't work out, we can always split,' if psychologically you don't entirely unpack your bags when you move in together, then I can almost guarantee that things won't work out for you. I appreciate the honesty implicit in your request, the desire not to live hypocritically. But you must understand that what a marriage commitment is all about is not just a mutual willingness to sleep with each other, but a commitment to accept the frustrations and disappointments that are an inevitable part of two imperfect human beings relating to each other. It's hard enough to make a go of marriage even when you give it everything you've got. But if part of you is involved in the relationship and part of you is standing outside it, evaluating it, deciding whether it's still worth it, then you have virtually no chance."

Those young people had been frightened by the pain they had seen others go through when marriages failed. They were so afraid of losing their emotional investment that they were willing to commit only a little bit of themselves to the relationship. That way, if it did not work out, it would not hurt them so much to lose. But the result would almost inevitably be a fragile, tentative relationship that was so "undercapitalized" in an emotional sense that it was sure to fail.

I think of all the letters I have received from women who told me that when they became seriously ill or learned that they had a seriously ill child, their husbands left them. I don't believe that all those husbands and fathers were cruel, callous, unfeeling people. On the contrary, I suspect that they felt the pain of the situation very deeply, and because nobody had ever taught them how to live with pain, they could not handle it. So they panicked and ran away from a threatening, emotionally overpowering situation. Perhaps some of them, like the young couple in my study, entered into marriage expecting it to make their lives pleasurable, and when it seemed to offer pain, conflict, and uncertainty instead of pleasure, they decided this was not the bargain they had contracted for and they got out.

Dr. Hendin contrasts the fairy tale of the frog prince,

where the beautiful princess kisses the frog and it turns into a handsome prince, with the version he saw one day on "Sesame Street," where she kisses it and turns into a frog herself. A funny scene, but is it teaching our children at some level that intimacy, emotional giving is dangerous and can leave you hurt?

If we believe that in order for life to be good, we have to avoid pain, the danger is that we will become so good at not feeling pain that we will learn not to feel anything —not joy, not love, not hope, not awe. We will become emotionally anesthetized. We will learn to live our whole lives within a narrow emotional range, accepting the fact that there will be few high spots in our lives in exchange for the guarantee that there will be no low moments either, no pain or sadness, just a perpetual feeling of monotony, one gray day after another. Because of our fear of pain, we will have mastered the art of detachment so well that nothing will be able to reach us emotionally.

The affliction which drains so much of the sense of meaning from our lives these days is the disease of *boredom.* So many of us find our jobs boring, our marriages boring, our friendships and hobbies boring. In pathetic desperation, we look for a movie, a vacation trip, an outlet of some sort to lift our lives above the level of the mundane. Some of us will find ourselves doing all sorts of potentially self-destructive things, driving too fast, hang gliding, white-water rafting, because "only then do I feel alive." Some people will turn to drugs in a desperate effort to rise above the emotional flatness of the everyday and learn what it feels like to feel again. A generation ago, drugs were the escape mechanism of the ghetto, an alternative to hopelessness and despair, a way to stop feeling the pain. Today, with a commensurate rise in price, they have become the plaything of the jaded upper middle class, not to relieve the pain but to escape the boredom, to feel high and feel good and experience heightened sensations of sight and sound and touch, because nothing in the real world gives them that feeling.

The teenager who shoplifts or steals cars and ends up with a police record and the housewife who drifts into an extramarital affair and ruins her marriage and her reputation may not be trying to do something wicked and harmful. They may just be looking desperately for something to add excitement to their otherwise humdrum, boring lives. Like Faust, they are prepared to sell their souls to the devil in exchange for one moment of feeling alive.

We keep thinking that the fault is in what we are doing or with whom we are doing it, and that the cure for the plague of boredom is to change jobs, to change mates, to change neighborhoods, and life will become more interesting. Sometimes a change may in fact be called for, but often the problem is in ourselves. Because of our fear of being hurt or being disappointed, we have chosen a life of emotional flatness. We have built for ourselves an emotional floor below which we will not sink, to make sure that nothing ever hurts or depresses us, and an emotional ceiling beyond which we cannot rise, because then the risk of falling would be too great, and we wonder why we feel so hemmed in. We inject ourselves with a spiritual novocaine so that we can walk through the storms of life and never be hurt, and we wonder why we feel so numb.

One of the fairy tales collected by the Brothers Grimm is entitled "The Tale of the One Who Went Forth to Learn Fear" (*The Juniper Tree,* L. Segal and M. Sendak; Farrar Straus Giroux, 1973). It is about a young boy who, no matter what he does, never feels afraid. He feels incomplete without the emotional dimension of fear. So he goes out and has many hair-raising adventures, encountering ghosts and witches and fire-breathing dragons, but never feels even a shudder. In his last adventure, he frees a castle from a wicked spell, and in gratitude the king gives him his daughter in marriage. The hero tells his bride that, although he is fond of her, he is not sure he can marry her until he completes his mission of learning to feel fear. On their wedding night (at least in the version the Brothers Grimm tell to children), his wife pulls back the covers and throws a bucket of cold water full of little fish over him. He cries out, "Oh my dear wife, now I know what it is to shudder," and he is happy.

What is this strange tale about? As interpreted by Bruno Bettelheim in his book *The Uses of Enchantment,* the story seems to imply that a person is not really grown up and ready for adult life, no matter what he or she may have accomplished in the world, until he or she is emotionally mature and open to feeling. Our hero cannot feel love or joy until he is able to feel fear and dread. He is perhaps a symbol of all of us who, in our efforts to avoid being hurt, deaden ourselves to all feeling and, unlike the hero of the fairy tale, don't even know what we are missing.

SIX

"But the Fool Walks in Darkness"

SEVERAL summers ago, moviegoers of all ages were enchanted by the story of E.T., the extraterrestrial. Telling the story of a creature from a more advanced civilization who was accidentally stranded on earth, it rapidly became one of the best loved and most profitable films of all time. Much of the movie pits the children, who simply want to love E.T. and be loved by him, against the scientists, who want to capture him and study him. Now, the conflict between free-spirited youngsters and authority-minded adults is as basic to movies as the conflict between cops and robbers or cowboys and Indians. But *E.T.* added something new to the story. The villains in *E.T.* are not simply grown-ups trying to enforce rules. They are scientists who are out to make love disappear in the name of scientific progress.

(A year later, the movie *Splash* told essentially the same story. A mermaid comes to dry land looking to love and be loved, and scientists want to capture and dissect her.)

On the one hand, human beings' ability to reason has been our crowning glory. Philosophers from the time of Aristotle have identified it as the quality that makes us different from animals. When the opening pages of the Bible describe Adam as naming the animals, tribute is being paid to his unique ability to reason, to sort things into categories. Man alone can use his mind to make tools, to build machines, to change his environment, as well as to write books and symphonies.

But on the other hand, our reason tells us that reason itself has its limits. If you dissect a frog, you will have a lot of information about how frogs are put together, but you won't have a frog anymore. If you dissect and analyze a mermaid or an extraterrestrial visitor, you may well gain a scientific breakthrough and maybe even win a Nobel Prize, but you will no longer have a friend who loves you, and for a lot of people, the gain in information is just not worth it. The biblical Hebrew verb *yada*, "to know," somewhat like the English word "understand," can mean either to have information about someone or something, or to be intimate with someone. But it seems that we have to choose between analyzing someone at a distance and getting so close that we experience the other person rather than intellectually understanding him or her.

Ecclesiastes, grown too old and too cynical for a life of pleasure, turned to philosophy in an effort to discover the meaning of life, and found himself "understanding" life instead of living it. He read all the books, heard all the learned lectures, and what he learned was that the meaning of life is not to be found in philosophy. Having a lot of information about how to live is like having a lot of information about swimming or music but never going in the water or picking up a violin.

In June of 1985, I was invited to address the graduating class of Cornell University. I said to them that if the average graduating senior was twenty-one or twenty-two years old, most of the Vietnam War had happened while they were children, too young to understand what was going on. So the irony of the phrase "the best and the brightest" was lost on them. "The best and the brightest" was the way we described the government officials who got us into Vietnam to begin with and then kept getting in deeper and deeper. They were undeniably brilliant men, honor graduates of the finest universities, armed with mountains of information from the most sophisticated computers, and still they kept making the wrong decisions. They had intelligence. They had information. But they lacked wisdom, the instinctive sense of how to apply the information they had.

And the essence of wisdom, I suggested, was a respect for the limits of human intelligence and a sense of reverence for the vast dark reaches of reality where reason cannot penetrate.

If their Ivy League education had developed their minds but had let their sense of humility and reverence atrophy, I told them, they would run the risk of being "the best and the brightest" of their generation, smart enough to lead but not wise enough to know where they should be going. Some of them would be going on to medical school, and I expressed the hope that they had learned not only chemistry and biology, but also a sense of reverence for the miracle of life and the wondrous complexity of the human body. I hoped that they had learned that some ailments cannot be cured by brilliant diagnosis and elaborate machinery, but only by loving and caring. Without that humility and reverence, they might end up practicing the equivalent of auto mechanics on human beings, but they would never cure.

Some of them would become successful in business, and I warned them of the day when intelligence unaided by sensitivity, the mind without the heart, computer print-outs and rational decision making, would lead them to make decisions that would unnecessarily hurt people. At a time like that, I told them, reverence for the human soul should be more important to them than attention to the bottom line.

As a result of seeing where intellectually gifted leaders had taken us, as a result of other large and small calamities of the twentieth century (from seeing the most cultured nation in Europe launch the Holocaust to seeing the most creative scientists among us spoiling our air and our drinking water), we have learned to mistrust intelligence as a guide to life. The teachings of Sigmund Freud color the thinking of all of us in the twentieth century, reminding us that we may think we are acting out of logical reasons but we probably do the things we do for reasons we cannot understand.

Ecclesiastes set out to test the truth of the proverb he had heard all his life, "The wise man has eyes in his head but the fool walks in darkness." He hoped he would learn that it was true. He needed the reassurance that it is better to be wise than to be foolish, better to be learned than to be ignorant. He needed the conviction that in much learning, he would find the key to living, and that the uneducated person would be left to drift through life without a compass. After all, he was a wise, thoughtful person, a cultured man, a good student. Would that be enough to keep his life from slipping inevitably toward death and oblivion? Would being wise rather than foolish really make a difference?

But he learned only that if the wise man has eyes to see, what he sees is the limited usefulness of being wise. Perhaps Ecclesiastes saw, as we have seen so often, smart people doing foolish things. Consider the implication of the word "rationalize." To rationalize means to do something wrong, and then invent reasons to justify it. We use our intelligence not to figure out the right thing to do, but to make clever excuses for having done the wrong thing.

Perhaps Ecclesiastes saw bright people using their intelligence as a way of avoiding emotional commitment, analyzing rather than caring, like the scientists who would rather "understand" E.T. than let themselves love him. If the wise man walks in daylight and the fool in darkness, are there some things which are spoiled by exposure to the light? Are some of life's pleasures meant to be experienced without being analyzed and understood? A classic cartoon shows an exasperated teenager telling her mother, "For Pete's sake, will you stop understanding me!"

Perhaps the fool does walk in darkness, but half of our lives are spent in darkness, in the nighttime hours, and it may be that we have to learn to spend part of our lives as "fools," giving ourselves over to emotions we do not entirely understand and cannot control, so that we can live comfortably in that darkness. I know people who are as afraid of being openly emotional as many people are afraid of the dark. Love, joy, rage frighten them because they feel out of control. They cannot let themselves get angry, they cannot lose themselves in love, because that would mean losing control of their emotions, and that frightens them. They have trouble handling emotions which do not make sense. (The ancient fable of Pandora's Box tells of a woman, Pandora, who is given a sealed box by the gods and is told never to open it. Of course, Pandora is curious and opens the box, and all sorts of demons escape. It occurs to me that the story need not be an account of how women brought trouble into the world. Might it not rather be a parable of how men try to keep the emotional sides of their personalities locked up because they consider them dangerous, while women are less frightened of them? In Greek, *Pandora* means "many gifts.")

There is a tradition in both Judaism and Christianity of the "holy fool," the simple, uneducated, unsophisticated person who serves God spontaneously and enthusiastically, without stopping to think about what he is doing. His serving is especially beloved because no intellectual barriers come between him and his God. One of the most beloved stories of medieval Christianity is the story of the Lady's Juggler. Every one of the faithful was coming to bring his or her gift to honor the Virgin on her holiday. They were fine, expensive gifts, handwoven tapestries, jewel-encrusted crowns. One poor, simple young man had no present to bring and no money with which to buy one. But he could juggle. So he danced and juggled before the statue of the Virgin, to the horror of all the very proper spectators, and because his juggling was from the heart, it was the most acceptable gift of all.

If we are going to spend part of our lives walking in darkness, shall we do it conscious of all the dangers that may be lurking there, or shall we walk as "fools," realizing that we do not have all the answers and that it is not always up to us to find the way? There have been two world wars in this century, and countless other smaller wars, and tens of millions of people have been killed in them. Most of those wars were planned and executed by reasonable, intelligent men. Small wonder then that after every war, we become disillusioned with reason and intelligence and where they lead us. In recent years, we have seen a resurgence of fundamentalism and extremism, and a celebration of the irrational, in Christianity, Judaism and Islam. We have seen the appearance of yarmulkes on the heads of Jewish students on college campuses and veils on the faces of female students in the Middle East. Though their symbolism is very different, they are both ways of rejecting the modern world and its values, including its claim that the human mind, unaided by God, can discover the truth. We have seen the emergence of faith healers and evangelists on television to an unprecedented degree, and millions of people seem to be receptive to their message that it is the "best and the brightest" who walk in darkness, and only the irrational, the "fools for God," who have eyes to see.

Was Ecclesiastes disappointed by what he learned about the ability of the mind to plot his course through life? He never seems to give up his faith in reason. He never becomes mystical nor does he trade his skepticism for a religiously fundamentalist outlook. And after all, he does end up writing a book on the subject. But he seems to be saying, "I have learned it all. I have gone as far as reason can carry me, *and it is just not enough.* I need more. I need the kind of truth that reason cannot lead me to, but I am a logical, reasonable person and I don't know where to find it. Physicians and philosophers talk to me about life and death, and when I listen to them, it all makes so much sense. But if it makes sense, *why am I still so afraid of dying and disappearing?*" One suspects that if he ever finds an answer to that question, the answer will be one which does not make sense, at least not on a rational level.

Many years ago, when I was young, a business associate

of my father's died under particularly tragic circumstances, and I accompanied my father to the funeral. The man's widow and children were surrounded by clergy and psychiatrists trying to ease their grief and make them feel better. They knew all the right words, but nothing helped. They were beyond being comforted. The widow kept saying, "You're right, I know you're right, but it doesn't make any difference." Then a man walked in, a big burly man in his eighties who was a legend in the toy and game industry. He had escaped from Russia as a youth after having been arrested and tortured by the czar's secret police. He had come to this country illiterate and penniless and had built up an immensely successful company. He was known as a hard bargainer, a ruthless competitor. Despite his success, he had never learned to read or write. He hired people to read his mail to him. The joke in the industry was that he could write a check for a million dollars, and the hardest part would be signing his name at the bottom. He had been sick recently, and his face and his walking showed it. But he walked over to the widow and started to cry, and she cried with him, and you could feel the atmosphere in the room change. This man who had never read a book in his life spoke the language of the heart and held the key that opened the gates of solace where learned doctors and clergy could not.

The human mind is a great thing, perhaps the most indisputable proof of God's hand in the evolutionary process. When you realize that human beings are born weaker, slower, more naked, and more vulnerable than so many other creatures, you come to understand that it is only by applying our intelligence to the world that we are able to survive. Where other animals have fur and feathers, we have learned how to weave clothes and heat our homes. Where other animals have developed massive muscles, we have built machines. The human mind has created medicines and invented artificial hearts to prolong life. It has written books which can inspire us and make us more compassionate. But it has its limits. There are questions, including some of the most important questions, which it is probably incapable of answering. As Pascal put it, "The heart has its reasons which reason cannot know."

When I was a seminary student, the student body was divided into two camps: the rationalists, who approached the tradition with their minds, as something to be understood and explained; and the mystics, who approached the same tradition with their souls, as something that could never be understood or explained but only experienced. I was strongly in the rationalist camp in those days. We looked down on the others as medieval mystifiers who would never be taken seriously by a congregation of college graduates. They dismissed us as bearers of a dry, arid legalism which would never reach beyond the top three inches of a person, enlightening the mind but never engaging the soul. We rationalists believed back then that if we could explain religion to people and show them how it made sense, they would be persuaded. After all, we would be dealing with intelligent, reasonable people. Why shouldn't they listen to reason? We failed to understand that faith, like love, loyalty, hope, and many of the most important dimensions of our lives, is rooted in that vast, dark, irrational area where reason cannot reach and man's intellect cannot venture.

Adlai Stevenson once wrote:

What a man knows at fifty that he did not know at twenty is, for the most part, incommunicable. All the observations about life which can be communicated handily are as well known to a man at twenty who has been attentive as to a man at fifty. He has been told them all, he has read them all, but he has not lived them all. What he knows at fifty that he did not know at twenty is not the knowledge of formulas or forms of words but of people, places, actions, a knowledge not gained by words but by touch, sight, sound, victories, failures, sleeplessness, devotion, love —the human experiences and emotions of this earth and oneself and other people; and perhaps too a little faith and a little reverence for things you cannot see" (quoted in William Attwood, *Making It Through Middle Age*, Atheneum, 1972, p. 107).

Today, I am twenty-five years older and wiser, and in fulfillment of Jung's prediction that in mid-life we go back and fill in the spaces we left blank when we were growing up, I find myself quoting Judaism's mystical tradition as much as its rational one. Time and again, I turn to books I had no patience for during my student days. I have come to appreciate the value of customs and rituals that "don't make sense." There is a cycle of daylight and darkness, of mind and emotion in my inner world even as there is in the world around me. Sometimes our life's task is to shed light where there is darkness, to make sense of the things that happen around us, to find connections and explain them. But sometimes our life's task is to accept the darkness, the things which cannot and perhaps should not be explained, as part of the world we live in.

At the end of the movie, E.T. escapes from the high priests of science and reason who are chasing him and heads into the darkness to go home. At the end of *Splash*, the mermaid and her earthling lover similarly outrun the police and the scientists and escape into the dark undersea world. And in the end, we too will one day go off into the darkness, and if we have learned how to live, we will face it neither wisely nor foolishly, but bravely and unafraid.

SEVEN

---❧---

Who's Afraid of
the Fear of God?

I CAN picture Ecclesiastes as a man growing older, desperately sensing that he is beginning to run out of time, too honest to repress or deny his fears and gripped by the sense that he will soon come to the end without ever having done something meaningful with his life. To be sure, he has been rich and his life has been a pleasant one, but those are such transient things. Riches can disappear in one's own lifetime or slip from one's grasp at death. Rich people can be obnoxious, lonely, sick. And all those moments of pleasure disappear as soon as they are over. In the end, he knows that he will have to face the darkness alone, without either his wealth or his pastimes to protect him. And if he will be asked, by himself or by someone else, "What did you do with your life, with all the opportunities and advantages that you had?" what will he answer? That he made a lot of money, read a lot of books, and went to a lot of parties? A person's life should add up to more than that.

Ecclesiastes at this point in his life is wise and well read, learned enough to know that there is no answer in all of his learning to the question that haunts him. One day, he will write a book to try and answer it. But before he can do that, he has one more path to pursue. Desperate to do something with his life which will be not only successful and pleasant but *right* in an enduring sense, he leaps beyond the limits of knowledge and understanding, trying to reach the far shore where reason cannot lead him. Growing older and more frustrated daily, Ecclesiastes, like many people as they grow older, turns to religion. From now on, there will be no more doubting or questioning. Ecclesiastes will devote himself wholeheartedly to the service of God and the doing of His will.

Human beings do not live forever. That, of course, has been the starting point of Ecclesiastes' entire search and the rock on which all of his hopes were shattered. What was the point of being rich or wise when rich people and poor people, wise men and fools are all fated to die and be forgotten? But God is eternal; He is forever. If we attach ourselves to the Eternal God and devote our lives to His service, might that not do the trick? Might that not be a way of cheating death and avoiding that sense of futility and finality which makes all of our strivings meaningless? Ecclesiastes sets out to do things which are eternally right and true, hoping in that way to gain eternity.

He never tells us why it did not work. Maybe he was too much of an individualist to be satisfied by the prospect of dying and disappearing himself but having served eternal values. Maybe he found hypocrisy and meanness in the halls of religion, learning that the most outwardly pious can be inwardly rotten, and came to doubt the worthwhileness of piety. He writes at one point (8:10) of seeing scoundrels being given honored burials in the shadow of the Temple, while virtuous but humble people lay forgotten and unattended. Maybe he was just too old to change the critical, skeptical habits of a lifetime. But whatever the reason, we soon find him saying, "Be not overeager to go to the House of God." (4:17) "Do not overdo goodness or act the wise man to excess, or you may be dumfounded. Do not overdo wickedness or be a fool, for you may die before your time. It is best that you grasp the one without letting go of the other." (7:16–18) In other words, let your life be a mixture of piety and sinfulness; all things in moderation! Piety alone apparently was not the answer.

It is a devastating thing to have God fail you. However you conceive of God and whatever names you give Him, to base your life on certain assumptions and then to have them collapse under you is a shattering experience. It leaves you feeling not only that your theology is not right but that nothing in the world is right. Take God out of the picture, let events force a person to admit that the fundamental assumptions of his life are false, and the whole world seems meaningless. I think of the idealistic intellectuals of the 1920s and 1930s who gave themselves heart and soul to the Communist party, and who tried for years not to notice its cruelty and hypocrisy. When they finally had to confront the truth about the cause they had worked so hard to serve, it was more than an education or a disappointment. It was the destruction of the moral basis of their lives. (In fact, a book about disillusioned ex-communists is entitled *The God That Failed.*) In Camus' novel *The Plague,* the priest Paneloux tells his congregation repeatedly that the outbreak of bubonic plague in their city is God's judgment on them for their sins and that ultimately God works all things for the best. When an innocent child dies in agony shortly thereafter, Father Paneloux himself falls ill and dies almost immediately afterward, not so much from the plague, one suspects, as from the experience of having the principles to which he had devoted his whole life proven false. Without that support, how could he live? His God had failed him.

Ecclesiastes' God has failed him too. He had turned to God looking for security, for serenity, for freedom from fear and doubt by placing himself in the service of God. It was probably not his fault that he did not find what he sought and needed in religion, and it was certainly not God's fault that Ecclesiastes turned to religion looking for the wrong things. The fault, if there was any, may have been in the nature of religion as it was understood back then.

In the Bible, there is no word for "religion." The concept is too abstract. The phrase closest in meaning to it is "the fear of God." What do those words "the fear of God" mean to you? Do they conjure up the picture of an all-powerful authority living in heaven and thundering His will down to us, ready to smite us if we disobey? Do they make you think of a God who knows your every secret thought and deed, and will punish you if you do wrong ("putting the fear of God in you")? If so, then you are like a lot of people today and throughout the ages, whose understanding of religion has been based on fear of punishment. Religion becomes a matter of God's commanding and our obeying and being rewarded, or else disobeying and being punished. This was the way most people in Ecclesiastes' day understood religion. ("If you follow My laws and faithfully observe My commandments, I will grant you rains in their season . . . you shall eat your fill of bread and dwell securely in your land . . . But if you do not obey Me and do not observe all these commandments, . . . I will wreak misery upon you, consumption and fever. You shall sow your seed to no purpose for your enemies shall eat it." Leviticus: 26) And this was why Ecclesiastes could find no satisfaction when he tried to make religion the cornerstone of his life. He may have been sufficiently ahead of his time to sense that a life of obedience based on fear was not what he was searching for.

I have to introduce the important philosophical point of this chapter with a personal story. In 1961, I was a chaplain in the United States Army, stationed at Fort Sill, Oklahoma. I had been east for a conference and was flying back to Oklahoma from New York, changing planes in Chicago. The flight out of New York was delayed; I missed my connection in Chicago and would have to wait several hours for the next plane. At that point, I realized that I had just about finished reading the book I had brought along and had a two-hour wait and a two-hour plane ride ahead of me. Robert Louis Stevenson once defined an intellectual as someone who could spend an hour waiting for a train with nothing to read and not be bored. I guess I don't qualify; I needed a book to fill those hours. I tried the paperback bookstand at O'Hare Airport. Virtually the only book that didn't feature a half-naked woman on the cover was something entitled *The Moral Judgment of the Child* by Jean Piaget. I had never heard of Piaget or his book before, but rather than board the plane with my chaplain's insignia and a lurid novel, I decided to buy it. The book and its ideas went on to become one of the forces reshaping my life and thought, and I sometimes wonder to what extent my life would have been different had my plane left LaGuardia on time instead of forty minutes late that day.

Jean Piaget was a Swiss psychologist who was fascinated by the question of how children grow mentally. At what age do they start to understand concepts of "mine" and "yours"? What do they understand about time and space, about truth and make-believe at various ages? His research had led to a shelfful of books on the process of thinking in children.

The Moral Judgment of the Child deals with a child's concept of right and wrong, permitted and forbidden. Piaget had a disarmingly simple way of gathering data. He would go out onto the streets of Geneva, approach children playing marbles, and ask them three questions:

How old are you?
How do you play marbles?
How do you know that is the way to play?

What he came away with was the attitude of children at various ages to rules of any kind, to religious and secular authority, to the seriousness of breaking rules and the procedures for changing them. Piaget discovered three stages in the evolution of a child's sense of authority.

Young children see the rules of a game, and by extension all the rules they are given, as having been handed down by an unquestionable higher authority. This is how you are supposed to play/behave, and it never occurs to them to do things differently. Piaget would ask these young children, "Why do you have to do it that way? Suppose you played the game some other way?" They would stare at him uncomprehendingly and say, "But that's not right. If you did that, you wouldn't be playing marbles." Rules are rules, and one becomes part of the system by accepting and obeying them.

As children grow older and approach adolescence, Piaget found, they begin to question those rules, as indeed they begin to question all authority. Now they don't have to be prompted by an adult's question. They themselves say, "Who says we have to do it that way? It's our game; why can't we make any rules we want?" Typically, children then go through an irresponsible phase, inventing a lot of silly rules, sometimes making the game too easy until it is not fun anymore, sometimes making it impossibly hard, before coming to the conclusion that they do have the power to make and change rules, but the rules they invent have to be fair and reasonable, or else playing the game won't be any fun.

At this point, says Piaget, they are at the threshold of maturity. They understand that the rules don't come from "on high." Rules are made by people like themselves, tested and perfected over the course of time, and can be changed by people like themselves. Being "good" no longer means simply obeying rules. It now comes to mean sharing in the responsibility of evaluating and making rules which will be fair to all, so that we can all enjoy living in a fair and just society.

Piaget suggests that these attitudes toward a game of marbles are a paradigm of our attitudes toward all rules, all authority. When we are young and weak, we picture the source of rules as being all-powerful and all-knowing. We show our appreciation for guidance by accepting and obeying the rules. A "good" child is not necessarily a generous or morally sensitive child but a docile and obedient one. At this stage, we have difficulty accepting the idea that other people, other cultures, other religions have different rules than we do. If we are right and they are different, they must be wrong. We are the norm; they are "funny" or exotic if they eat differently, dress differently, or pray differently than we do. Wearing rings in our ears is what normal people do; wearing a ring in your nose is bizarre.

Children enter into adolescence, and they are suddenly no longer interested in being "good." Obedience, winning the approval of their parents, is no longer their highest value. Like Piaget's second-stage subjects who did some silly things with their marbles until they realized that really wasn't all that much fun, adolescents do a lot of foolish things, sometimes hurting themselves or others, in the process of showing off how free of rules they can be. As anyone who has raised teenagers knows, they will reject good advice rather than be in the position of listening to parents and other authority figures. That is their notion of being "free."

Then, if they are lucky, they grow to become responsible adults, men and women whose definition of "good" has come to mean more than obedience. It now means evaluating and adjusting the rules, using their power in the interest of fairness.

I read Piaget's book on the plane to Oklahoma that night and read it again when I arrived home. I realized that he was not only describing how the individual human soul grows morally. He was giving us, perhaps without even realizing it, a guide to the history, and perhaps the future development, of the two great centers of authority in our societies, politics and religion.

Doesn't the history of human government resemble Piaget's scheme of the history of a single child playing marbles? In the beginning there were absolute rulers and obedient subjects. Monarchs held absolute sway, with the power to make and enforce laws, to decree and collect taxes as they saw fit. Loyalty to the ruler, being a law-abiding citizen, serving in the army and paying your taxes without complaint were the only real civic virtues. People obeyed their king, usually not because they loved him— How could they? They hardly knew him—or because they believed he wanted what was best for them, but because they feared his power.

Then there were revolutions against the absolute power of rulers, often leading to periods of chaos and excess, with many innocent victims suffering from the arbitrary and unfair application of justice, corresponding to Piaget's second, adolescent stage. That revolutionary chaos gave birth to democracy, the idea that all the people should be involved in making the laws, so that the laws would reflect their collective will and wisdom. Rulers ruled only by the choice and consent of the people as a whole.

And what has been the history of religion, the ways in which we understood God, over the course of generations? Once God was pictured as an absolute monarch, a King of Kings. He would tell us how to live, and we would show ourselves as good people by obeying Him, living by His word. He would reward us for unquestioning devotion and punish us for being unfaithful servants. Every community would have its religious leaders and specialists, people who spoke for God and knew His will, and the faithful would feel obliged to obey them. God and His human representatives never had to explain themselves. They had only to decree, and people would follow.

Then at about the same time that people were beginning to question the divine right of kings and to insist on being given a voice in running government, they began to question the divine right of God, as it were. They began to see the Bible as an inspired document written by human hands, rather than dictated by God. They saw certain laws and customs as resulting from the cultural and economic circumstances of the people who fashioned them, rather than having come directly from the mind of God. People no longer wanted to think of themselves as "faithful servants." They wanted to be God's children grown to maturity. Parallel to the emergence of political democracy in Europe and America, people began to assert their right to "vote" on matters of faith and morals as well.

I have been fascinated by the impact that the American environment has had on Protestant, Catholic, and Jewish religious traditions brought to these shores by immigrants from Europe. Authoritarian religious strictures were forced to yield to the American creed of "This is a free country and nobody is going to tell me what to do." Churches which emphasized local, "democratic" control —the Baptists, Congregationalists, and Unitarians— flourished more than the centralized, hierarchically controlled churches that had been powerful in Europe. American Catholics felt free to transgress the teachings of their church leaders and still think of themselves as good and loyal Catholics. Jews abandoned Orthodoxy for the less demanding voice of Reform, or responded to the Conservative teaching that religion was shaped by the people, not imposed by the leaders. Like Piaget's marble shooters on the sidewalks of Geneva, religious communities evolved from the stage of being docile, obedient children through an adolescent period of rejection and rebellion into a community of free adults demanding a voice in setting the rules by which they would live.

Piaget would insist that he is not simply showing us a range of options, alternative patterns of moral behavior. The later stages are better, more fully moral behavior than the earlier stages, even as an adult is more fully developed and more mature than a child. No matter how cute and charming a child might be, there is something incomplete about him. In that sense, democracy and power sharing are not just matters of Western taste like baseball and cheeseburgers. They represent a higher, more complete, more moral form of social organization than dictatorship. Living patterns behind the Iron Curtain, for example, where the government controls everything and people are in constant fear of the authorities, are objectively less moral because they represent a less mature, more childish stage of development. Those early stages may be appropriate for a young child, even as it is appropriate for a young child to want to live with his parents and have other people make decisions for him. But there is something flawed about a person who never outgrows those childish notions and patterns as he grows older.

And it is here that Piaget has something to teach us not only about the mind of a child but about the future of religion and the quest for the good life. We learn from him that *obedience is not necessarily the highest religious virtue.* A religion that defines morality as obedience to its commands is appropriate to children and immature people, and may have been appropriate to humankind as a whole when civilization was immature. The Bible may speak in terms of "Thus says the Lord"; it may promise rewards to the righteous and punishment to the wicked, because it was addressed to people in the earliest stages of their moral development. The Bible may well be the Word of God, but it may not be His final word not because God's ability to express Himself was limited but because people's capacity to understand Him was. A religion which persists in understanding "good" to mean "unquestioningly obedi-

127

ent" is a religion which would make perpetual children of us all.

I have known people who were deeply serious about their religion, people whose religious commitment was the single most powerful force in shaping their lives, and who nonetheless left me wondering whether all that religion was good for them. In some cases, there was a frantic obsession with sin, a perpetual fear that they had inadvertently broken some rule, done something wrong and offended God, losing their Heavenly Father's love. In others, there was an attitude of "Now God will see how good and devoted I am and maybe He will finally love me." I have known Jews who would spend the Sabbath not in serenity and spiritual refreshment, but in constant concern that they might be doing something forbidden, until the day became a weekly ordeal to be survived. I have known Christians who could not watch a television commercial without worrying that they were having lustful thoughts about one of the models, or who feared that they were guilty of the sin of pride anytime someone complimented them on what good examples they were to the community. Every action was undertaken in a spirit of "Now God will see what a good person I am and He will love me." I could not help feeling that there was something incomplete about their attitudes, that their interpretation of religion was somehow keeping them from growing up.

There is a part of us that wants to remain a child. When Peter Pan sings about not wanting to grow up and assume adult responsibilities, the children in the audience, all of whom can hardly wait to be a year older, think he is strange but the adults understand perfectly (and of course, it was an adult who wrote the original play and another adult who added that song). There is a part of us, especially in times of stress, that wants to be cuddled and taken care of, to be told, "There's nothing to worry about; I'll take care of everything for you." How often have I seen a patient in a hospital, a man who might be a business executive, a woman whose days are ordinarily one long string of decisions to be made and responsibilities to be borne, revert to an almost childlike "Take care of me" attitude. There is a part of us that wants somebody else to step in and do all the hard things we are supposed to do, relieving us of responsibility. A medieval Spanish monk wrote in his journal, "I am confident that, after my death, I will go to heaven because I have never made a decision on my own. I have always followed the orders of superiors, and if ever I erred, the sin is theirs, not mine."

In the same vein, the psychologist Erich Fromm, after fleeing from Nazi Germany to the United States, tried to understand how a cultured, educated people like the Germans could have let a man like Hitler come to power. In his book *Escape from Freedom,* he suggests an answer. Sometimes, he says, the problems of life become so overwhelming that we despair of ever solving them. Should someone come along and say in a loud, confident voice, "Follow me without question, do everything I tell you to, and I will lead you out of this," many of us would find that a very tempting offer. When life becomes difficult, we want someone to say to us, "Don't worry your little head about it. Let me do it for you, and all I want in return is your gratitude and total obedience."

That wish for someone to step in and take over when life starts to get complicated is the child in us speaking from our adult bodies. When religion panders to that wish, when religious leaders keep us in childlike submission and dependence, telling us what to do and asking our obedience and gratitude in return, it does us a disservice. This is where the religion of Ecclesiastes' day failed him. Authentic religion should not listen to us when we say, "This is too hard. Tell me what to do so that I don't have to figure it out for myself." It should urge us to grow, to leave childish patterns behind even if we would rather remain spiritual children. Religion should even encourage us to challenge its own positions critically not out of adolescent impatience with limits but on the basis of an informed adult conscience. ("Encourage" is such a good word. Religion should not be in the position of giving us answers. It should give us courage to find our own way.)

My job as a rabbi would be a lot easier if I could expect people to obey me in whatever I told them to do, as my job as a teacher would be easier if students would write down and memorize everything I said without questioning. But in both cases, I would be shortchanging the people who looked to me for enlightenment. People are more like plants to be nurtured rather than empty vessels to be filled with my surplus wisdom. We can ask *children* to be obedient. "Don't play with that!" is more appropriate than a lecture on the dangers of starting a fire or the consequences of breaking an antique heirloom. But we should stop treating adults as if they were still children in the name of religion. Ultimately, morality has to mean more than obedience.

The fear of God may indeed be the beginning of wisdom and the cornerstone of proper living, as the Bible repeatedly states. But "the fear of God" does not mean being afraid of God. "The fear of God" is not fear as we use the word today, but awe and reverence. Fear is a negative emotion. It is constricting. It makes us either want to run away from whatever we are afraid of, or else want to destroy it. It makes us feel angry and resentful, angry at the person or thing that frightens us and angry at our own weakness which leaves us vulnerable. To obey God out of fear is to serve Him sullenly and with only part of ourselves.

But awe is different. The feeling of awe is similar to fear in some ways. We feel a sense of being overwhelmed, of confronting someone or something much more powerful than ourselves. But awe is a positive feeling, an expansive feeling. Where fear makes us want to run away, awe makes us want to draw closer even as we hesitate to get too close. Instead of resenting our own smallness or weakness, we stand openmouthed in appreciation of something greater than ourselves. To stand at the edge of a steep cliff and look down is to experience fear. We want to get out of that situation as quickly and safely as we can. To stand securely on a mountaintop and look around us is to feel awe. We could linger there forever.

Ecclesiastes, at the end of his religious phase, may well have said to God, "What more do You want of me? I have groveled, I have offered You unquestioning obedience, I have done everything You asked me to. Why then have You withheld from me that sense of completeness, that promise of eternity that I was looking for?" And God may have answered, "What pleasure do you think I take in your groveling? Do you really think I am so insecure that I need you to diminish yourself to make Me feel great? I wish people would stop quoting what I said to the human race in its infancy, and listen to what I am trying to tell them today. From children, and from spiritual children, I expect obedience. But from you 'unquestioning obedience' is just another name for the failure to act like an adult and take responsibility for your own life. Do you want to feel complete? Do you want to feel as if you have finally learned how to live? Then stop saying, 'I only did what You told me to,' and start saying, 'You may or may not like it, but I have given it a lot of thought and this is what I feel is right.' "

True religion should not say to us, "Obey! Conform! Reproduce the past!" It should call upon us to grow, to dare, even to choose wrongly at times and learn from our mistakes rather than being repeatedly pulled back from the brink of using our own minds. For responsible religious adults, God is not the authority telling them what to do. God is the divine power urging them to grow, to reach, to dare. When God speaks to such people, He does not say, as one might to a child, "I will be watching you to make sure you don't do anything wrong." He says rather, "Go forth into an uncharted world where you have never been before, struggle to find your path, but no matter what happens, know that I will be with you." Like a father who is genuinely proud when his children achieve success entirely on their own, God is mature enough to derive pleasure from our growing up, not from our dependence on Him.

Authentic religion does not want obedient people. It wants authentic people, people of integrity. What is integrity? The word "integral" means whole, undivided, all of one piece. Living with integrity means finding out who you are and being that person all the time. Religion does not expect us to be perfect. That not only would be impossible, setting us up for inevitable failure. It would almost be antireligious. If we were perfect, we could never learn (that would imply there was something we were lacking before). We could never grow or change. We would have no need for religion, and in our perfection, we would be as great as God. But religion can expect us to be whole in another sense, not flawless but constant. The young have a word for it. They speak of a person being "together" in the sense of knowing who one is and what one stands for. (A thought: When we speak of one God, are we doing something more than taking a census of how many divine beings there are? Are we perhaps saying that God "has it together," that He is a symbol of constancy and unvarying integrity? Maybe we can't be as wise, as powerful, or as good as God, but we can strive to be as *whole* as He is.) The challenge of authentic religion is not for us to be perfect, but for us to get ourselves together and be at all times who we are at our best.

As the parent of a teenager and frequently the teacher of adolescents, I know how quick teenagers are to denounce hypocrisy in their parents and their religious and political leaders. One of the most dismissive names they can call someone is a "phony," a person who says things he or she does not mean or who claims to believe certain things but acts differently. I am not about to come out in favor of hypocrisy, but I do find myself wondering why young people get so much more indignant about such discrepancies than they do about other equally serious issues (being cruel to the weak, for example, or taking things that don't belong to them). I suspect that it is because hypocrisy and integrity are big issues for them during their formative years. Adolescence is such a volatile time. Young people can be studious and respectful at one moment, impatient and boisterous an hour later. They can be terribly idealistic in the afternoon as they visit a nursing home or raise money to combat world hunger, and appallingly selfish and self-centered on a date a few hours later. Adolescents by definition are going through the process of finding out who they are, and it is a very uncomfortable thing for them to be so changeable. I can imagine that, in order to survive, they have to believe that in a few more years they will have resolved these issues and taken permanent shape. At fifteen, they say to themselves, I may be confused and inconsistent, but by the time I am twenty, I should be the same person all day every day. That is why it is so upsetting for them to find out that even older people, well-respected people have not achieved that sense of integrity. That is why one of the goals of the fully realized person is to develop this sense of integrity.

Religion is not a nagging parent, nor is it a report card keeping track of our achievements and failures and grading us for our performance. Religion is a refining fire, helping us get rid of everything that is not us, everything that distorts, dilutes, or compromises the persons we really want to be, until only our authentic selves remain. God's first words to Abraham, "Go forth out of your land, your birthplace, your father's house, to the land which I will show you," can be understood to mean, "Follow Me and obey Me without question." But they can also mean, "Leave behind all the influences that keep you from being the person you are capable of being, so that the real Abraham can emerge."

What is a person of integrity like? There is a Yiddish word which is untranslatable but describes him or her perfectly, a *mensch*. To be a mensch is to be the kind of person God had in mind when He arranged for human beings to evolve, someone who is honest, reliable, wise enough to be no longer naive but not yet cynical, a person you can trust to give you advice for your benefit rather than his or her own. A mensch acts not out of fear or out of the desire to make a good impression but out of a strong inner conviction of who he or she is and what he or she stands for. A mensch is not a saint or a perfect person but a person from whom all falsehood, all selfishness, all vindictiveness have been burned away so that only a pure self remains. A mensch is whole and is one with his or her God.

I have known people of integrity, and the impression they leave is memorable. There is a quiet confidence to them, a sense of tranquility that comes at the end of the process of figuring out who you are and what you stand for. Unlike anxious religious people who are consumed by the fear that they may have broken some rule and offended God, men and women of integrity are concerned with living up to their own high standards, not with offending or pleasing God. Yet in their presence, one feels that God has reason to be pleased.

Father Robert F. Drinan was my representative in Congress for several years. He was an articulate spokesman for compassion and liberalism. Because he had been a Roman Catholic priest and dean of a law school before being elected to Congress, his voice was listened to when he spoke out on moral and ethical issues, and he seemed to relish the opportunity to shape American law and life. But when word came down from Rome forbidding priests from holding political office, Robert Drinan stepped aside when his term was over and did not seek reelection. A reporter asked him if he had considered defying the order to get out of politics and he answered, "Oh no, I could never do that." Some people thought that he was simply living up to his vows to obey his superiors, that he was saying he could not think for himself once the order had been given. But I think I understood what he was saying. He was saying that he knew who he was. Being a Jesuit priest was the core of his identity; everything else, however enjoyable or gratifying it was, was secondary. He could not do anything to betray or conflict with that core. Had he tried to be a Jesuit sometimes and a Congressman sometimes, he would have lost the sense of integrity which comes with being the same person at all times and which was the secret of his strength. Like a photograph which is slightly out of focus, there would now be two images of him, just far enough apart from each other that we would no longer be able to see the person clearly.

With this insight, we are beginning to move from Ecclesiastes' last questions to the beginnings of his answer. Ecclesiastes turned to religion to make him whole, to help him lead a life of enduring meaning. But the religion of his time, because it demanded obedience rather than authenticity, because it offered more fear and less awe, could not make him whole. It could make him "good" in the sense of obedient, but that was not what he was looking for. He needed more from God than that, and because he would not give up the search for it, he finally found it.

EIGHT

❧

Go Eat Your Bread
in Gladness

Y OU may remember the Hassidic tale mentioned in chapter 2, about the man who was lost in the forest and met another wanderer who told him, "I am lost too. But we can tell each other which paths we have already tried and been disappointed in. That will help us find the one which leads out."

That was where we began. We accompanied Ecclesiastes on five well-traveled paths that turned out to be dead ends, the way of selfishness and self-interest, the way of renouncing all bodily pleasures, the way of wisdom, the path of avoiding all feeling in an effort to avoid pain, and the path of piety and religious surrender. The wise old man who wrote the Book of Ecclesiastes began by telling us of his disappointments. Neither wealth nor learning nor piety gave him the satisfaction of knowing that his life would mean something, not in his lifetime nor beyond it. But he did not write his book only to share his frustration with us nor was it included in the Bible to persuade us that life is in fact pointless. Ultimately, Ecclesiastes has an answer and he shares it with us in these words:

Go, eat your bread in gladness and drink your wine in joy, for your action was long ago approved by God. Let your clothes always be freshly washed and your head never lack ointment. Enjoy happiness with a woman you love all the fleeting days of life that have been granted you under the sun. Whatever it is in your power to do, do with all your might. For there is no doing, no learning, no wisdom in the grave where you are going. (9:7–10)

It is a strange answer, not one we would have expected from him. Has he given up? Is he reduced to saying to us, "Eat, drink, and be merry for who knows how long you will live? Go have a good time since nothing lasts and nothing matters anyhow." I don't think he is. "Eat your bread in gladness and drink your wine in joy" may sound a lot like "Eat, drink, and be merry" but coming from Ecclesiastes, I suspect that it means something very different. I suspect that he is saying something like this: I have examined all the evidence and come to the conclusion that nothing endures and nothing makes a difference. Everything is vanity. Human beings are born and die like flowers or insects and that is all there is to it. The evidence leads me to conclude that life has no meaning. *But there is something inside me which will not permit me to accept that conclusion.* My mind tells me that the arguments for the meaninglessness of life are overwhelming: injustice and illness and suffering and sudden death, criminals getting away with murder while good people die in shame and poverty. My mind tells me to give up my quest for meaning because there isn't any. All of my experience points in the same direction. But something from deeper inside me wells up and overrules my mind, dismissing the evidence, and insists that in spite of all, a human life has to mean something. And that feeling, says Ecclesiastes, is why I am a human being and not an animal.

A friend of mine once tried to persuade me that the issue of God's permitting evil was irrelevant because we define evil from a human point of view, not from God's vantage point. He said to me, "If frogs wrote theology, they would ask why an all-powerful, loving God did not create more swamps and more mosquitoes." I answered him, "Yes, but you're missing the essential point. Frogs don't write theology but people do. Frogs don't question the meaning of life but people do, because there is a divine dimension, a bit of God's image in every one of us, which moves us to ask questions like, Why are we alive? That is why the death of a child is a tragedy while the death of a tadpole is not."

If logic tells us that life is a meaningless accident, says Ecclesiastes at the end of his journey, don't give up on life. Give up on logic. Listen to that voice inside you which prompted you to ask the question in the first place. If logic tells you that in the long run, nothing makes a difference because we all die and disappear, then *don't live in the long run.* Instead of brooding over the fact that nothing lasts, accept that as one of the truths of life, and learn to find meaning and purpose in the transitory, in the joys that fade. Learn to savor the moment, even if it does not last forever. In fact, learn to savor it *because* it is only a moment and will not last. Moments of our lives can be eternal without being everlasting. Can you stop and close your eyes and remember something that happened for only a moment or two many years ago? It may have been a view of a spectacular landscape, or a conversation that made you feel loved and appreciated. In a sense it did not

141

last very long at all, but in another sense it has lasted all those years and is still going on. That is the only kind of eternity this world grants us. Can you close your eyes and conjure up the memory of someone who is now dead but once meant a lot to you? Can you, in your mind, hear her voice and feel her touch? There is proof that a person, by learning how to live, can cheat death and live on beyond her allotted years.

When we stop searching for the Great Answer, the Immortal Deed which will give our lives ongoing meaning, and instead concentrate on filling our individual days with moments that gratify us, then we will find the only possible answer to the question, What is life about? It is not about writing great books, amassing great wealth, achieving great power. It is about loving and being loved. It is about enjoying your food and sitting in the sun rather than rushing through lunch and hurrying back to the office. It is about savoring the beauty of moments that don't last, the sunsets, the leaves turning color, the rare moments of true human communication. It is about savoring them rather than missing out on them because we are so busy and they will not hold still until we get around to them. The author of Ecclesiastes spent most of his life looking for the Grand Solution, the Big Answer to the Big Question, only to learn after wasting many years that trying to find one Big Answer to the problem of living is like trying to eat one Big Meal so that you will never have to worry about being hungry again. There is no Answer, but there are answers: love and the joy of working, and the simple pleasures of food and fresh clothes, the little things that tend to get lost and trampled in the search for the Grand Solution to the Problem of Life and emerge, like the proverbial bluebird of happiness, only when we have stopped searching. When we come to that stage in our lives when we are less able to accomplish but more able to enjoy, we will have attained the wisdom that Ecclesiastes finally found after so many false starts and disappointments.

Corita Kent, the former nun turned graphic artist, says in one of her posters, "Life is a series of moments/to live each one is to succeed." We misunderstand what it really means to be alive if we think that we can solve the problem of living once and for all by acquiring wealth, acquiring an education, acquiring a suitable husband or wife. We never solve the problem of living once and for all. We can only deal with it day by day, a constant struggle to fill each day with one day's worth of meaning. This, ultimately, is Ecclesiastes' insight and advice to us. Our author looked in vain for the key to the meaning of life. Try as he might, he could never find it. But despite his repeated failures, he could not bring himself to conclude that life was meaningless. He saw and felt the futility, the injustice of so much that happens to us on earth. But at the same time, he sensed that life, however muddled and frustrating, was too sacred, too special, too full of possibilities to be meaningless, even though he could never find that meaning. At last, he found it not in a few great deeds but in thousands of little ones.

A star football player interviewed on the eve of the Super Bowl was quoted as saying, "If this is the Ultimate Game, how come they're going to play another one next year?" We could similarly say, If we could do something today which would permanently and finally answer the problem of living, what would we need tomorrow for?

Why would God have to create a tomorrow? Life is not a problem to be solved once; it is a continuing challenge to be lived day by day. Our quest is not to find the Answer but to find ways of making each individual day a human experience.

When the children of Israel left Egypt, God sought to impress them with a miracle so spectacular that no one who experienced it would ever doubt His power or His providence again. He caused the waters of the Red Sea to part, letting the Israelites pass through in safety and releasing the waters to drown the Egyptian pursuers. Safely across the sea, the people were suitably impressed and sang God's praise, pledging Him their undying loyalty: "The Lord will be our King forever and ever." God's plan worked—for about forty-eight hours. By the third day after the crossing, the people were hot, tired, and thirsty. They complained to Moses about the lack of food and water and wondered why they ever let themselves in for this in the first place. God realized that no matter how impressive a miracle might be, it does not solve the problem of faith for more than a day or two, any more than the finest meal solves the problem of being hungry for very long. So God changed His tactics. Instead of a spectacular miracle once a generation, He provided the Israelites with water to drink, manna to eat, and shade to rest in every day. As the people "ate their bread in gladness," they experienced the goodness of God and the fullness of life in the everyday, unspectacular miracles which made their lives bearable. In the same way that a half-hour of exercise every day does more to keep us fit than six hours of exertion once a month, a few small experiences of the meaningfulness of life every day will do more for our souls than a single overwhelming religious experience.

* * *

I remember reading an interview once with an eighty-five-year-old woman from the hill country of Kentucky, who was asked to look back over her life and reflect on what she had learned. With that touch of wistfulness that inevitably accompanies any statement beginning "If I had it to do over . . . ," she said, "If I had my life to live over, I would dare to make more mistakes next time. I would relax. I would be sillier, I would take fewer things seriously . . . I would eat more ice cream and less beans. I would perhaps have more actual troubles but fewer imaginary ones. You see, I'm one of those people who lived seriously and sanely hour after hour, day after day. I've been one of those persons who never went anyplace without a thermometer, a hot water bottle, a raincoat, and a parachute. If I had it to do again, I'd travel lighter."

"Go eat your bread in gladness." "More ice cream and less beans." Less wealthy and less well educated than the author of Ecclesiastes, the woman from Kentucky feels, like him, that she has wasted too much of her life following the wrong advice and wants to keep us from making the same mistake. She has come to understand how easily the pleasures of life today are spoiled by worry about what might happen tomorrow. She has learned how fear can banish joy, making us tense with apprehension, and how laughter can chase fear and set us free. And she wants to pass those lessons on to us.

"Go eat your bread in gladness and drink your wine in joy, for your action was long ago approved by God." In a world where not everyone will do great deeds or achieve great success, God has given us the capacity to find greatness in the everyday. Lunch can be a hurried refueling, the equivalent of an auto racer's pit stop, or it can be an opportunity to savor the miracle that dirt, rain, seeds, and human imagination can work on our taste buds. We just have to be wise enough to know how to recognize the miracle, and not rush headlong past it in our search for "something important." We can smile at the adolescent girl mooning over her new boyfriend. She may think that the most wonderful thing in human history has just happened to her, while we know it is just another set of glands ripening on schedule and in six months she will wonder what she ever saw in him. Yet there is something touching about being able to be made so happy by a letter, a phone call, or a smile. There is a capacity for finding joy in the ordinary which we might well envy. The good life, the truly human life is based not on a few great moments but on many, many little ones. It asks of us that we relax in our quest long enough to let those moments accumulate and add up to something.

A rabbi once asked a prominent member of his congregation, "Whenever I see you, you're always in a hurry. Tell me, where are you running all the time?" The man answered, "I'm running after success, I'm running after fulfillment, I'm running after the reward for all my hard work." The rabbi responded, "That's a good answer if you assume that all those blessings are somewhere ahead of you, trying to elude you and if you run fast enough, you may catch up with them. But isn't it possible that those blessings are behind you, that they are looking for you, and the more you run, the harder you make it for them to find you?" Isn't it possible indeed that God has all sorts of wonderful presents for us—good food and beautiful sunsets and flowers budding in the spring and leaves turning in the fall and quiet moments of sharing—but we in our pursuit of happiness are so constantly on the go that He can't find us at home to deliver them?

Ecclesiastes' advice to look for lots of small answers in the middle of life rather than One Big One leads him to point us toward another source of potential fulfillment, our work. "Whatever it is in your power to do, do with all your might." Work hard, not solely because it will bring you rewards and promotions but because it will give you the sense of being a competent person. Something corrosive happens to the souls of people who stop caring about the quality of their work, whatever that work may be, and begin to go through the motions. Some jobs can afford to be done poorly and no one will be hurt, but none of us can afford the internal spiritual cost of being sloppy in our work. It teaches us contempt for ourselves and our skills.

When we take our newfound enthusiasm for finding pleasure in the moment, and apply it not only to our leisure time and vacations but to our work as well, we find yet another important area of giving fullness and meaning to the way we spend our time. Novelist Wallace Stegner has written that from the Garden of Eden, where Adam and Eve were punished with hard labor, condemned to earn their bread by the sweat of their brows for their disobedience, to the gates of Auschwitz which were inscribed *Arbeit macht frei,* "Work sets one free," work has gotten a bad press. Yet, he goes on to say, "More people than would probably admit it find in work the scaffolding that holds up their adult lives." Freud identified love and work as the two things that the mature person has to be able to do well. We work because we need the money. But we work for other reasons as well. How often have you read about the mail carrier, truck driver, or secretary who wins the lottery and becomes an instant millionaire, but continues to get up at six in the morning to go to work, because work is what they do and who they are. Asked, "What do you do?" we invariably respond in terms of our work, not our hobbies or organizational commitments.

I work because I have a family to support and bills to pay. But I work also because it puts me in touch with people and helps me think of myself as a competent, contributing person. There have been times, all too often in my professional life as a clergyman, when in the course of twenty-four hours I will offer an opening prayer at a senior citizens' program on Sunday afternoon, conduct a wedding on Sunday night, meet with my staff or attend a professional meeting on Monday morning, and at noon on Monday officiate at the funeral of a young wife and mother who died of cancer, going on to spend much of the afternoon with the bereaved family. The funeral is by far the least pleasant of all those activities, the one at which I feel the most inadequate. And yet in a strange way, I feel good when I am officiating at a funeral. For years, I never understood that feeling. I thought there might be something perverse about me, to enjoy such moments. But I understand it now. At times like that, I feel alive and engaged. I know that I am not merely present but that I am making a difference. I do not like to officiate at funerals of young people and I would prefer to do it less often, but there is something satisfying about being challenged to do something hard and then doing it. I think that must have been what Ecclesiastes had in mind when he said to us, in effect, "If you are not going to win a Nobel Prize for your work, if it is not going to make you rich and famous, it can still give meaning to your life if you take it seriously and do it with all your might."

If we are lucky, we will find ourselves at a place in life where we can derive pleasure from our work. Some of us will have had a vision early in our lives of what we wanted to spend our energies doing, and it will have worked out for us. Being a doctor, a lawyer, a teacher is as gratifying as we dreamed it would be. Some of us, if we are lucky, will see ourselves launched on new careers in mid-life which will give us that elusive feeling of pleasure: the college-educated woman whose children are now old enough that she can go out and do what she always thought she would be good at; the middle-management executive who can let go of the dream of being rich and powerful, cash in his stock options, and earn a living using the gardening skills which had been his hobby for years; the accountant who opens a restaurant and is happier getting up before dawn as his own boss than he ever was reporting to an office at nine o'clock. And most of us will continue to show up for work at the same address day after day, year after year. But the key to our happiness, to our being able to find pleasure in our work, is the sense that we are using our abilities, not wasting them, and that we are being appreciated for it. "Whatever it is in your power to do, do with all your might."

It is terribly frustrating to know that you can do something and not be called on to do it, or to believe that you can do it and never have the chance to find out. So the track star takes two years off from work to train for the Olympics, not because it makes economic sense but because he has to find out how good he is at the highest level of competition. The factory worker promoted to a desk job takes off his jacket and fixes a broken machine because he is proud of the fact that he can do it, and can't stand seeing less skilled people botch up the job. The frustration of the professional athlete with a lucrative contract but a seat on the bench, like that of the surplus worker who knows she will get paid even if there is no work for her to do, testifies to the fact that we work for meaning as much as for money. We work so that our days will not be empty of meaning.

It should be pointed out that "whatever it is in your power to do" does not refer only to the things we get paid for. We do many things on a volunteer basis because we want that feeling, which our nine-to-five jobs may not be giving us, of using our skills, making a difference, and being appreciated. So the assembly-line worker coaches a Little League team and knows the satisfaction of teaching, advising, and making decisions. The secretary sings in the church choir or staffs a crisis-center hot line, where she gains the feeling of being depended on and having people look up to her. My synagogue, like churches, synagogues, lodges, and civic organizations across the country, offers opportunities for volunteers to plan programs, chair committees, organize fund-raising events, speak in public, and enhance the fortunes of an organization they cherish, while at the same time gaining the feeling of putting their hidden talents to use.

Sometimes in life we have to become less to be more. We become whole people, not on the basis of what we accumulate, but by getting rid of everything that is not really us, everything false and inauthentic. Sometimes to become whole, we have to give up the Dream.

The Dream is the vision we had when we were young —perhaps planted by parents or teachers, perhaps flowering from within our own imaginations—that we would be somebody truly special. We dreamed that our names would be famous, that our work would be recognized, that our marriages would be perfect and our children exemplary. When things do not turn out that way, we feel like failures. We will never be happy until we stop measuring our real-life achievements against that Dream. We will never be comfortable with who we are until we realize that who we are is special enough. If we have succeeded in becoming authentically human, eating our bread in gladness and enjoying life with people we love, then we do not have to become rich and famous. Being truly human is a much more impressive accomplishment. In *Seasons of a Man's Life*, Dr. Daniel Levinson sees middle adulthood as offering the opportunity to renounce the "tyranny of the Dream" and become successful on more realistic terms. He writes, "When a man no longer feels he must be remarkable, he is more free to be himself and work according to his own wishes and talents."

At one point, the sages of the Talmud say something remarkable. They say, "One hour in this world is better than all of eternity in the World to Come." What do they mean? I take that passage to mean that when we have truly learned how to live, we will not need to look for rewards in some other life. We will not ask what the point of righteous living is. Living humanly will be its own reward. The person who has discovered the pleasures of truly human living, the person whose life is rich in friendships and caring people, the person who enjoys daily the pleasures of good food and sunshine, will not need to wear herself out in pursuit of some other kind of success. No praise or promotion from strangers, no fancy car or lofty title could ever match the happiness she already knows.

The story is told of the factory that had a problem of employee theft. Valuable items were being stolen every day. So they hired a security firm to search every employee as he left at the end of the day. Most of the workers willingly went along with emptying their pockets and having their lunch boxes checked. But one man would go through the gate every day at closing time with a wheelbarrow full of trash, and the exasperated security guard would have to spend a half-hour, when everyone else was on his way home, digging through the food wrappers, cigarette butts, and Styrofoam cups to see if anything valuable was being smuggled out. He never found anything. Finally one day, the guard could no longer stand it. He said to the man, "Look, I know you're up to something but every day I check every last bit of trash in the wheelbarrow and I never find anything worth stealing. It's driving me crazy. Tell me what you're up to and I promise not to report you." The man shrugged and said, "It's simple. I'm stealing wheelbarrows."

We totally misunderstand what it means to be alive when we think of our lives as time we can use in search of rewards and pleasure. Frantically and in growing frustration, we search through our days, our years, looking for the reward, for the success that will make our lives worthwhile, like the security guard looking through the trash in the wheelbarrow for something of value and all the while missing the obvious answer.

When you have learned how to live, life itself is the reward.

NINE

———❧———

Why I Am Not
Afraid to Die

A FRIEND of mine, a clergyman I admire, turned to me once with a problem. A member of his congregation, a forty-two-year-old doctor, was hospitalized with an inoperable brain tumor. My friend said to me, "I don't know why, but I just can't bring myself to visit him. I like him, I care about him, I know how much my visits mean to him, but I keep finding reasons not to go and see him, and it bothers me." I told him, "I think I understand why you do that. I suspect that you see too much of yourself in him. Seeing him ill and dying makes you think that a year from now, it could be you in that situation, and you can't handle that. I would guess that you are afraid of dying—it's nothing to be ashamed of; lots of people are—and that is why seeing someone your own age dying is so hard for you to deal with."

"How do you get over the fear of dying?" he asked me. I told him that I was not ready to die, that I hoped to live for many more years, but that I was not afraid of dying because I felt satisfied with what I had done with my life. I had the sense that I had not wasted it, that I had lived with integrity, had done my best, and had an impact on people which would outlast me. I pointed out to him that he could certainly say the same things about himself, about his life and his work, that he had already reached the level of living humanely. It is only when you are no longer afraid to die that you can say that you are truly alive.

I believe that it is not dying that people are afraid of. Something else, something more unsettling and more tragic than dying frightens us. We are afraid of never having lived, of coming to the end of our days with the sense that we were never really alive, that we never figured out what life was for.

Of all the fears that haunt us, from fear of the dark when we are young to fear of snakes and high places, there is nothing to compare to the fear that we may have wasted our lives with nothing to show for it. I have attended many people at the end of their lives. Most of them wanted to live longer if they could. They did not want to leave their loved ones. But they were not afraid of death because they knew that they had had time to live and they had used that time well. Virtually the only people I have known who were afraid of dying were people who thought that they had wasted their lives. They would pray that if God would only give them another few years, they would use them more wisely than they had used all the years up till then. I can think of no punishment for a wasted life more frightening than that, and no reward for a life well lived more gratifying than the sense that you accepted the challenge to be human and were up to it.

There is a story told of a man who died after having led a thoroughly selfish, immoral life. Moments later, he found himself in a world of bright sunlight, soft music, and figures all dressed in white. "Boy, I never expected this," he said to himself. "I guess God has a soft spot in His heart for a clever rascal like me." He turned to a figure in a white robe and said, "Buddy, I've got something to celebrate. Can I buy you a drink?" The figure answered, "If you mean alcoholic beverages, we don't have any of that around here." "No booze, huh? Well then, what about a game of cards? Pinochle, draw poker, you name it." "I'm sorry but we don't gamble here either." "Well, what do you do all day?" the man asked. "We read the psalms a lot. There is a Bible class every morning and a prayer circle in the afternoon." "Psalms! Bible study all day long! Boy, I'll tell you—heaven isn't what it's cracked up to be." At which point the figure in white smiled and said, "I see that you don't understand. We're in heaven; you're in hell."

Heaven, the story suggests, is having learned to do and enjoy the things that make us human, the things that only human beings can do. And by contrast, the worst kind of hell I can imagine is not fire and brimstone and little red figures with pitchforks. The worst hell is the realization that you could have been a real human being, you could have been a mensch, and now it's too late. You could have known the satisfaction of caring for another person, of being generous and truthful and loyal, of having developed your mind and your heart, of controlling your instincts instead of letting them control you, and you never did it.

"Who shall ascend into the mountain of the Lord and who shall stand in His holy place? One who had clean hands and a pure heart." (Psalm 24:3–4) "Ascending the mountain of the Lord" doesn't necessarily mean going to heaven after you die, nor need it refer to going to church or synagogue (though the original reference in the psalm was probably to visiting the Temple of Jerusalem). Climbing the mountain of the Lord can mean growing to full humanity in this life, using your years well, living with "clean hands and a pure heart," so that even while you are alive, you will have that feeling of "standing in His holy place." When you have done that, even the prospect of death will hold no terror for you.

Many years ago, I saw a scene from a play on television, and I have never forgotten it. A young man and a young woman are standing at the railing of an ocean liner. They have just gotten married, and this cruise is their honeymoon. They are talking about how fulfilling their love and marriage have been for them, even beyond their expectations. The young man says, "If I were to die tomorrow, I would feel that my life had been full because I have known your love." His bride says, "Yes, I feel the same way." They kiss and move away from the rail, and now the audience can see the name of the ship on a life preserver: TITANIC.

If people in biblical times grew old at about the same rate that we do today (and there is reason to believe that they did; the ninetieth psalm says the average person lives to age "threescore and ten," that is, about age seventy, and the exceptional person to age eighty), then I can picture Ecclesiastes as a man in his mid- to late forties, perhaps close to fifty. He is at about the same point in his life that I am in mine. And he is beginning to be afraid that he is running out of time. The years ahead are almost certainly fewer than the years behind, and he still is not sure that he has done anything meaningful with his life. He may be looking back with regret on wasted times and wasted opportunities.

I sometimes think of this as the "instant coffee" theory

of life. When you open a jar of instant coffee, you dole it out in generous, heaping spoonfuls, because after all you have a whole full jar of it and you see that you are only using a little at a time. By the time you get down toward the bottom of the jar, you realize that you don't have all that much left, and your portions are more carefully measured. You reach after every last grain in the corner of the jar. I think we tend to treat time that way. Young people think that they will live forever. They assume that they have all the time in the world. They can afford to "invest" their time in activities that will not pay dividends until well into the future. They take entry-level jobs and low-paying apprenticeships as a foothold in the working world. They date people they know they will not marry because they are developing the skills of relating to another person.

But as we get older, halfway down the coffee jar, we learn not to be so casual with our time because we understand that it will not last forever. We stop asking the young person's questions—How high will I rise? How far will I get?—questions which are answered in terms of success and competition, and we start asking the questions which haunted the author of Ecclesiastes—What will I have accomplished? What difference will I have made? What will be left of me when my time is over?—questions which are answered on the basis of things shared with other people. It is a sign of maturity when we stop asking, What does life have in store for me? and start asking, What am I doing with my life?

Some examples of that process at work:

When I turned forty-five, I cut back on giving sermons and teaching classes and began to write books, as a way of bringing my ideas to people even when I was not physically present with them. Till then, I had dealt in spoken words, and words vanish as soon as you utter them. Without realizing it, I had begun to feel the need to express myself in a more permanent medium.

A friend of mine who owns a gas station, when he was in his early forties, changed the name of his station from "Maple Street Garage" to "Al Jones' Garage." Like me, he responded to middle age by wanting to see his name written on something permanent, not only in spoken words.

In January of 1984, Senator Paul Tsongas of my home state of Massachusetts announced that he would retire from the Senate and not stand for reelection that year. Tsongas was a rising star, an overwhelming favorite to be reelected, frequently mentioned as a potential candidate for Vice President or even President. A few weeks before his announcement, he had learned that he had a form of lymphatic cancer which could not be cured but could be treated and would probably not affect his physical abilities or his life expectancy. The illness did not force Paul Tsongas out of the Senate, but it did force him to confront the fact that he would not be around forever. He would not be able to do everything he might want to, so what were the things that he most wanted to do in the limited time that he had? Most of us manage to avoid that question; Paul Tsongas, waiting for word from his doctor, had to face up to it. He decided that what he wanted most in life, what he would not give up if he could not have everything, was being with his family and watching his children grow up. He would rather do that than shape the country's laws or get his name in the history books. He understood that if he was to have any sort of immortality, any sort of life beyond his years on earth, it would be rooted in that, not in his legislative accomplishments.

After he made his decision known, a friend wrote to congratulate him on having his priorities straight, adding, "Nobody on his deathbed ever said, 'I wish I had spent more time on my business.' " And of course Ecclesiastes, who was haunted by the same fear that there would not be enough time to do it all, said it first: "Go eat your bread in gladness and drink your wine in joy . . . Enjoy happiness with a woman you love all the fleeting days of life that have been granted you . . ." Paul Tsongas was forty-three years old when he made his decision.

If I were afraid of dying because I realized statistically that my life might well be two-thirds over and because I saw more people my age dying suddenly, I would have to live out my remaining years in fear and apprehension. As the author of the Twenty-third Psalm understood so many years ago, God does not redeem us from death. We will all die one day. But He redeems us from the *shadow of death,* from letting our lives be paralyzed by the fear of death. He helps us prevent death from casting its shadow over the years we do have to live.

The philosopher Horace Kallen marked his seventy-third birthday by writing, "There are persons who shape their lives by the fear of death, and persons who shape their lives by the joy and satisfaction of life. The former live dying; the latter die living. I know that fate may stop me tomorrow, but death is an irrelevant contingency. Whenever it comes, I intend to die living."

I have no fear of death because I feel that I have lived. I have loved and I have been loved. I have been challenged in my personal and professional life and have managed, if not a perfect score, at least a passing grade and perhaps a little bit better than that. I have left my mark on people and I have come to a point in life where I no longer need to leave my mark on people. I can look forward to the last act of my life, however long or short it may be, in the knowledge that I have finally figured out who I am and how to handle life. I walk unafraid through the valley of the shadow, not only because God is with me now but because He has guided me to this point. There is no way to prevent dying. But the cure for the fear of death is to make sure that you have lived.

In the previous chapter, we saw Ecclesiastes come to the same conclusion that Senator Tsongas did. A life of meaning is achieved not by a few great, immortal deeds but by a lot of little ones. The challenge is not to rise above the level of everyday life by some superhuman effort. The challenge is to find something truly human to do every day of our lives. When you realize that you do not have time for everything, when you find out that trying to cram everything into a twenty-four-hour day leaves you tired, leaves the things you do incomplete and half-baked, and leaves the people you share life with feeling that you never stop moving long enough for them to get to know you, what are the nonnegotiable elements of your life? What are the things you absolutely must have and do so that you can feel that you have lived your life and not wasted it? In our explorations of Ecclesiastes and of our own lives, we have identified three things:

Belong to people.
Accept pain as part of your life.
Know that you have made a difference.

We need to belong intimately to a few people who are permanent elements in our lives. Having a lot of casual acquaintances to talk sports or recipes with is no substitute. Just as "one chimpanzee is no chimpanzee," one human being cannot be completely and authentically human without ongoing relationships with a few people. And they have to be people with whom we share our whole lives, not just a fraction of our time and ourselves.

That is the reason, I suspect, why women tend to survive the emotional trauma of divorce or widowhood better than men do. Women tend to have close friends, people with whom they share their whole selves. Men tend to have acquaintances, business associates, people to bowl or carpool with, but people with whom they share only a part of themselves, not their whole selves.

When my previous book became a best-seller, I had the opportunity to give up the rabbinate and become a full-time writer and lecturer. It offered fame, travel, and more money for less emotionally demanding work. I chose to remain in my congregation, in part because being a rabbi is who I am, but in large measure because I intuitively realized that I needed to have the same people in my life on an ongoing basis. As a lecturer, I would be introduced to a lot of people I would never see again. I would give my talk, receive their applause, and leave town. If I am an effective speaker, I might say something which would remain with them, something which they would find helpful over the years. But I would not have a close, continuing relationship with any of them. As a congregational rabbi, I officiate at weddings of young women whom I have watched grow up since they were born. I counsel families whom I have known for years, with whom I have shared innumerable happy and sad moments. Just as our bodies have a need for air and food, our souls have a need to be connected to other people, not to be constantly surrounded by strangers. As one of my teachers used to say, "We do not appreciate what we receive, we appreciate what we share."

One of the memorable essays in the field of sociology in recent years was entitled "Portnoy's Mother's Complaint" by Pauline Bart. A young social worker describes her assignment of interviewing a fifty-year-old woman who has just been admitted to the hospital, suffering from severe depression. The woman was manifesting an extreme case of the "empty-nest syndrome." Her children had grown up and moved away, and she felt deprived of the only role that had ever given her life meaning. She had become so depressed that she had herself hospitalized. But what is fascinating about the interview is that "Mrs. Portnoy" (the doting but rejected mother) is not comfortable having the social worker asking her questions. She does not simply want to tell her story of how ungrateful and uncaring her children are. She insists on asking questions of the social worker: "Are you married? Why are you so thin? Do you live by yourself? Do you cook your own meals? You really ought to take better care of yourself, eat more fruit, get out in the fresh air. Here, would you like a chocolate?"

When she is asked to talk about her own life, "Mrs. Portnoy" comes across as apathetic and depressed. She sighs, she shrugs, there is no enthusiasm in her voice. But when she can turn the tables and "interview" the social worker, she becomes animated. She cannot get excited at the prospect of her children visiting her in the hospital or of getting a weekend pass to go home, but the prospect of going shopping to help the social worker buy a new dress excites her.

"Mrs. Portnoy" needs someone to mother. That is the only way she knows to define herself as a useful, competent person. She needs to be surrounded by people who need her and are grateful for her advice. When the last child struck out on his own, "Mrs. Portnoy" found herself "fired" from the only job she had ever known. Fifteen or twenty years sooner than it would happen to a man, she finds herself involuntarily retired from the commitments that gave her life meaning, and her depression and sense of worthlessness resemble the reactions of the older worker forced into retirement. That is why she responds as she does to the appearance of the young social worker. "If you really want to help me," she seems to be saying, "you won't help me by taking a case history and finding hobbies for me. You will help me by letting me adopt you as a daughter, fuss over you, worry about you, give you advice. I do it well, I need to do it, and frankly from the looks of you, you could probably benefit from it. So put away your notebook, stand up straight, don't wear so much makeup, wear brighter colors, take me home to cook some chicken soup for you. You'll see, we'll both be happier."

A life without people, without the same people day after day, people who belong to us, people who will be there for us, people who need us and whom we need in return, may be very rich in other things, but in human terms, it is no life at all.

I was sitting on a beach one summer day, watching two children, a boy and a girl, playing in the sand. They were hard at work building an elaborate sand castle by the water's edge, with gates and towers and moats and internal passages. Just when they had nearly finished their project, a big wave came along and knocked it down, reducing it to a heap of wet sand. I expected the children to burst into tears, devastated by what had happened to all their hard work. But they surprised me. Instead, they ran up the shore away from the water, laughing and holding hands, and sat down to build another castle. I realized that they had taught me an important lesson. All the things in our lives, all the complicated structures we spend so much time and energy creating, are built on sand. Only our relationships to other people endure. Sooner or later, the wave will come along and knock down what we have worked so hard to build up. When that happens, only the person who has somebody's hand to hold will be able to laugh.

To be fully and authentically human, we have to be prepared to take off the armor we usually go around wearing to keep the world from hurting us. We have to be prepared to accept pain, or else we will never dare to hope or to love. Without the readiness to feel, which must include feeling pain, we will never know the joy which Ecclesiastes identifies as one of the chief rewards of life. We have to make room in our souls for the tragic view of life. As long as we still insist on happy endings, we will still be children, upset and angry if God doesn't respond to our cries and make everything work out for us. I don't have very much good to say about suffering, but it does rob you of your illusions about how the world is supposed to work.

Our son Aaron was born the week that President John Kennedy was shot, and I remember a tearful Daniel Patrick Moynihan saying after the assassination, "When you're Irish, one of the first things you learn is that sooner or later this world will break your heart." It was one of the first things I had learned from Jewish history as well, and I would learn it more personally over the course of our son's brief life. I don't envy people who come into their forties without ever undergoing a serious illness, bereavement, or failure, because I know that sooner or later one will come their way, and I worry that they won't be able to handle it, never having had to do it before. The language of grief, the language of feeling anything, is like all languages. We learn them better when we are young. Like mumps or chicken pox, it is not much fun at any age, but if you have to go through it, you are better off going through it when you are young and developing a measure of immunity to it.

Why do hundreds of young people who seem to have so much to live for take their own lives every year? Why are there "epidemics" of teenage suicides, often in happy families, in affluent communities, incidents not necessarily born out of despair or hopelessness but seemingly random tragedies which leave families shattered and high schools and entire communities feeling haunted? More than any other tragedy, suicide leaves everyone feeling burdened and guilty, asking himself, "What could I have done to keep it from happening?" Yet such things are happening in increasing numbers throughout the country. The numbers, and the stories behind each incident, are truly tragic.

For that matter, why are middle-aged and older people driven to take their own lives, often when they find themselves faced with the prospect of serious illness or scandal? I suspect that the answer has to do with our society's attitude toward pain. From the outset, we have been told that for every pain, there was a pill we could take to make the hurting stop. In essence, we have been promised a pain-free life. When it does not work out that way, our inability to handle any strong emotion, especially pain, leaves us feeling confused and helpless, and we do not like feeling helpless. When something happens to hurt us and we cannot make the pain go away—illness, rejection, dreams that don't come true—we do not know how to deal with it. Sometimes we try to deny it, to pretend that it did not really happen or to pretend ("sour grapes") that it does not really bother us. When we are unable to fool ourselves, when the pain still hurts, we are at a loss. Never having learned to live with pain, some people see no other way out except to give up on living. Much mental illness is a way of fleeing from the pain of reality. Chronic alcoholism may often be an attempt to deaden the pain. But most tragic of all is the suicide of a person who is loved and talented and has much to live for, but forgets all that when he looks into the future and sees more pain than he is prepared to handle.

Yet pain is part of being alive, and we need to learn that. Pain does not last forever, nor is it necessarily unbearable, and we need to be taught that. Adolescents need to accept the fact that broken hearts, like broken bones, hurt dreadfully but ultimately they heal, and that there is life beyond the hurting. People whose shameful secret is about to be revealed need to be assured that there is forgiveness as well as condemnation, that there are people in the world and a God in the world capable of forgiving and loving even the most flawed and imperfect of us. The terminally ill need to be reassured that we will cherish them and spend time with them and take them as seriously as we did when they were healthy. Most of all, we have to learn to trust our own capacities to endure pain. We can endure much more than we think we can; all human experience testifies to that. All we need to do is learn not to be afraid of pain.

Grit your teeth and let it hurt. Don't deny it, don't be overwhelmed by it. It will not last forever. One day, the pain will be gone and you will still be there.

The final ingredient which enables us to say, "I have lived and my life mattered," is the knowledge that we have made a difference. Ultimately I suspect that is why Paul Tsongas chose to spend his time with his children rather than in the Senate. In politics, he could only hope to make some small lasting impact. At home, he knew that his influence would be substantial and permanent.

In what is probably the best psychological study done on the stages men go through as they grow up, *Seasons of a Man's Life* (Knopf, 1978), Dr. Daniel Levinson writes about the significant role of a *mentor*. A young man starting out in his career will benefit greatly if he has a mentor, an older patron, not old enough to be a father figure, but perhaps a half-generation older, someone who knows the ropes and will teach him how things are done, someone with enough prestige and influence to take a personal interest in his career. The young man or woman who finds such a mentor has a better chance of being successful.

Later in the book, Levinson looks at the process from the mentor's point of view. He writes:

Being a mentor with young adults is one of the most significant relationships available to a man in middle adulthood. The distinctive satisfaction of the mentor lies in furthering the development of young men and women, facilitating their efforts to form and live out their dreams . . . More than altruism is involved: the mentor is doing something for himself. He is making productive use of his own knowledge and skill in middle age. He is learning in ways not otherwise possible. He is maintaining his connection with the forces of youthful energy in the world and in himself. He needs the recipient of mentoring as much as the recipient needs him.

When I was forty-eight years old, I took a major step toward restructuring my work and my time. I persuaded the leadership of my congregation to reduce my responsibilities and bring in a full-time associate rabbi to share the teaching and pastoral burdens with me. I did this for two reasons. First, it would give me the time to write and lecture, to be with my family in ways that a full-time pastor often finds difficult. Second, it gave me the opportunity to be a mentor to a younger colleague, as I had been fortunate to have an older mentor when I began. I would have someone to pass my professional tricks of the trade on to, to see him grow as a result of my personal investment in him. Our daughter would be going off to college soon, and like "Mrs. Portnoy," I needed someone to guide and shape.

And so do we all. We all teach, officially and unofficially, not only the classroom teacher or college professor addressing a group of students, but the experienced bookkeeper or factory worker passing tips on to the new arrival, because having an impact on another person, shaping his or her life in some small but vital way, is one of the most enduring satisfactions we will know. We teach because we need to share. Erik Erikson has written that the challenge of these middle years is to choose between generativity and stagnation, between continuing to have an impact or sitting around waiting to die. The inability to generate can cause a person to become excessively involved with himself—his health, his popularity, his memories, his disappointments. Erikson goes on to say, "Man is so constituted that he needs to be needed, lest he suffer the mental deformation of self-absorption. Generativity is expressed in parenthood but also in work and creative thought. Man needs to teach." (Erikson, *Insight and Responsibility,* Norton, 1964, p. 130.)

If we think of life as a limited resource—a given number of years to live, *x* million breaths or heartbeats before our hearts give out—then every passing day or year brings us closer to the time when we will have none left. No wonder the prospect of growing older fills us with dismay. (A character in a short story I once read is asked why she has so little to say. She replies that each of us is born with a quota of words to speak in our lifetime, and when we use them up, we die.)

But suppose we could learn to see life not as the using up of a limited resource but as the accumulation of treasures. Every new friend we made, every new truth we learned or experience we underwent would make us richer than we ever were before. There is more to my life today than there was five or ten years ago because of all the ways in which I have grown and been enriched in that time. Mystery writer Agatha Christie's second husband was the archaeologist Lord Mallowan. Someone once asked her what it was like being married to an archaeologist, and she answered, "It's wonderful. The older I get, the more interested he is in me." You don't have to be an archaeologist to feel that way. The older we all get, the more interesting we become as people, because the experiences of the passing years have deepened and enriched us.

A friend once suggested that life was like a fine wine,

improving with age. I told him that what I did not like about that comparison was that, with every sip of the wine, there was that much less left. I would rather think of life as a good book. The further you get into it, the more it begins to come together and make sense. Characters become more fully developed, and the meaning of earlier incidents begins to become clear. And when we finally come to the end, there is a satisfying sense of completeness to it.

Life, if you will, is a work of art, and if we have paid loving attention to its details, we will be able to take pride in the finished product. How can an artist paint a picture or shape a statue, knowing that some stranger will buy it from her and she will have no way of knowing how much pleasure it gives its new owner? How can an author write a book which will be read by strangers living hundreds of miles away, and he will never know the impact it has on them? When we know the answer to those questions, we will understand why a person works so hard at living, at making something of his life, knowing full well that one day his life will be taken from him, and only other people will remain to remember how good it was.

The Talmud says there are three things one should do in the course of one's life: have a child, plant a tree, and write a book. They all represent ways of investing our creative, generative energy in things which will endure after we are gone, and will represent the best that was in us. They offer us the reassurance that our lives were not in vain, and that the world is indeed better for our having passed through it.

What gratifies me most about the success of my previous book is not the financial rewards it brought me or the fact that it has been translated into nine languages and was a best-seller in three foreign countries. Spy novels and gossipy biographies have done better than that. What gratifies me most is the experience of going to a city where I know no one and have never been before, giving a lecture, and having eight or ten people come up to me afterward to tell me, "Your book changed my life. I could never have made it through this past year without it."

Think one more time about the author of Ecclesiastes. He was so fearful that death would rob his life of meaning, making it as if he had never existed, that he had trouble finding pleasure in the pleasurable moments of his life. We don't know if he ever had children, but we know that he planted trees and gardens which people would be able to enjoy long after he was gone. And of course he wrote a book which continues to challenge and instruct people thousands of years later. What greater satisfaction, what greater promise of immortality could anyone want?

TEN

One Question
Left Unanswered

Among all my patients in the second half of life, that is, over thirty-five, there has not been one whose problem in the last resort was not that of finding a religious outlook on life. It is safe to say that every one of them fell ill because he had lost that which the living religions of every age have given their followers, and none of them has really been healed who did not regain his religious outlook.

—C. G. Jung,
Modern Man in Search of a Soul

I F there had been psychiatrists in Jerusalem twenty-five hundred years ago, Ecclesiastes might well have gone to one and told him, "I'm unhappy because I feel that something is missing in my life. I feel that I'm not as consistently good as I should be. I feel I'm wasting a lot of my time and my talents. I keep trying to live up to the standards I set for myself and sometimes I almost get there, but never quite. I feel that with all the advantages I have had, I have wasted my life." And the therapist might have told him, "You're asking too much of yourself. Be realistic, lower your standards. After all, you are only human." Ecclesiastes would have left the appointment feeling even more disappointed in himself for not being more comforted by such well-intentioned professional advice.

But it would probably have been the wrong answer. A man like Ecclesiastes needs to set his sights high. In order for his life to take on meaning, he has to feel that he has been summoned to do important things. We feel better when significant moral demands are made of us. We feel we are being taken seriously as moral creatures. It would have been better to tell him that God would forgive him for trying and falling short than to suggest that he give up the effort and lower his expectations of himself.

A young man who ran away from his conventional middle-class home to join the Unification Church was asked why he had done it. He replied, "My father only talks about getting into college and getting a good job. Reverend Moon talks to me about helping him save the world." Just as we misunderstand what it means to be a parent when we make life so easy for our children that they never have to test themselves, we misunderstand human nature when we think we are helping people by not expecting very much of them. "Only human" should not be an excuse for laziness, carelessness, or selfishness. To be human is a great thing, and God pays us the ultimate compliment when He makes demands of us that He makes of no other living creatures. It may be hard to be good, given all the distractions and temptations of the world, but it is a lot harder to be told that you don't have what it takes to be good, so you are excused from trying.

Ecclesiastes asked, "What makes my life matter? What makes it more than a passing phenomenon, not worth noticing while I am alive and destined to be forgotten as soon as I am dead?" His answer ultimately was, "I can't come up with an answer, but I instinctively feel that human life has to be more than mere biological existence. When I am happy at my work or with my family, when I love or am loved, when I am generous or thoughtful, I feel that something more significant than just being alive is going on. I feel human, and that feeling is more persuasive than logic or philosophy."

I think he is right, but he has not gone far enough. Having almost answered his question, "What makes my life matter?" by referring to instincts and vague feelings, he leaves one big question unanswered. In that case, who needs God? Can we deal with the issue of life's ultimate meaning without reference to God? Ecclesiastes has been disappointed by organized religion as he has been disappointed by pleasure, wealth, and learning. So he tries to build a foundation for his life all by himself, and he almost manages to do it. When he tells us to "eat [our] bread in gladness," he underscores his advice by adding, "for your action was long ago approved by God." Is there no more significant role for God in all this than to stand apart and approve of our actions from afar? Ecclesiastes has been a helpful guide, but he stops short of the one last step we need to take. Without it, our search for life's meaning may offer us no more than personal preferences and wishful thinking. Ecclesiastes has made a courageous leap of faith in the absence of any evidence that human life is meaningful, but it is only faith in himself to which he leaps. What will be the basis of his faith, the basis of his life's meaning, when he is no longer around to affirm it?

To what question is God the answer? When we suggest that God is the answer to, Does Somebody really live in Heaven? we trivialize religion and make it harder for thoughtful people to take it seriously and find help there. The existence of God is not the issue; the difference God can make in our lives is. When we claim that God is the answer to the question, Is Somebody up there watching me, keeping a book on all my sins and preparing a moral report card on me? we help fashion a religion grounded in fear and unrealistic expectations.

What does God do for us to lift our lives above the level of mere existence? For one thing, He commands us. He imposes on us a sense of moral obligation. Our lives become important because we are here on earth not just to eat, sleep, and reproduce, but to do God's will.

Human beings have a *need* to be good. We need to be taken seriously as moral agents, and God shows us that He takes us seriously by expecting moral behavior from us. We feel uncomfortable, inauthentic when we are not living up to our moral nature. That may be why little children who break something or do something wrong are not satisfied until they have been found out and punished. They do not want to get away with it. It may not be pleasant to be scolded or disciplined, but it is a whole lot worse to live in a world which does not care if you do good things or bad ones. This may also be why some church and synagogue congregations seem to enjoy "fire and brimstone" sermons in which the preacher scolds them for being such reprobates and sinners. It reassures them that God and His ministers have set high standards for them. It takes a lot to extinguish the spark of God in our souls and make us insensitive to the moral summons of being human. Even Hitler's SS troops needed periodic "sermons" to make sure that their instinct for compassion did not interfere with their work.

Our human nature is such that we need to be helpful, thoughtful, and generous as much as we need to eat, sleep, and exercise. When we eat too much and exercise too little, we feel out of sorts. Even our personalities are affected. And when we are selfish and deceitful, it has the same effect. We become out of touch with our real selves; we forget what it feels like to feel good.

Do you remember the story of Joseph from the Bible? When Joseph was seventeen, he was sold into slavery by his jealous brothers. His comfortable, secure life as his father's favorite was suddenly replaced by a life of hardship and insecurity. For twenty years, he dreamed of the day when he would get even with his brothers. He put up with loneliness and injustice by picturing in his mind's eye how he would make his brothers beg and grovel and plead for mercy, as they had made him do. And in his imagination, he loved every second of it.

Then one day it happened. There was a famine in the land of Canaan. Only in Egypt was there grain to be had. Joseph had become Pharaoh's minister of agriculture, in charge of distributing that grain, and it was in that setting that his brothers appeared before him. He recognized them but they did not recognize him. This was the moment he had been dreaming of for twenty years. Now he had them in his power. Now he would get even with them for what they had done to his life. But as he began to torment them, threatening to keep one of them as his slave and accusing them of being spies, something very strange happened. Joseph found that he was not enjoying it as much as he thought he would. It felt so good in his dreams to hurt them, to get even with them. But in actuality, he couldn't enjoy it. He did not like the person he was becoming. He who hated his brothers for being cruel and hardhearted could not stand seeing himself become cruel and hardhearted (and therefore a person worthy of being hated) like them (or rather, as they had been twenty years ago but no longer were). Joseph discovered that the human soul was not made for jealousy and revenge. Acting against his true nature, he became increasingly uncomfortable until finally he broke down and cried, and told his brothers who he was.

It may well be that selfishness, cynicism, mistrust of other people are not only immoral, offensive to God. They may be unhealthy and destructive to us as well. A 1984 study at Duke University Medical Center examined the link between "Type A behavior" (the impatient, hard-driving, highly competitive person) and heart disease. The hypothesis was that Type A personalities would develop coronary artery and blood pressure problems more than the average person. What they found instead was that some Type A personalities were healthier than the national average and seemed to thrive on the challenges and competition in their lives. But the Type A's who were competitive and aggressive because they believed that most people around them were cheats and liars and so they had to connive and lie to avoid being taken advantage of, were constantly tense and apprehensive, constantly at odds with the other people in their lives, and their arteries and blood pressure readings showed the results.

In the same way that the human body is fashioned so that certain foods and certain kinds of activity are healthier for us than others, I believe that God made the human soul in such a way that certain kinds of behavior are healthier for us than others. Jealousy, selfishness, mistrust poison the soul; honesty, generosity, and cheerfulness restore it. We literally feel better after we have gone out of our way to be helpful to someone.

God is the answer to the question, Why should I be a good and honest person when I see people around me getting away with murder? God is the answer not because He will intervene to reward the righteous and punish the wicked but because He has made the human soul in such a way that only a life of goodness and honesty leaves us feeling spiritually healthy and human.

Biologist Lewis Thomas has written that nature's great law for all living things is not the survival of the fittest but the principle of cooperation. Plants and animals survive not by defeating their neighbors in the competition for food and light but by learning to live with their neighbors in such a way that everyone prospers. God is the force that moves us to rise above selfishness and help our neighbors, even as He inspires them to transcend selfishness and help us. God pulls us upward out of ourselves, even as the sun makes the plants and trees grow taller. God summons us to be more than we started out to be.

Recently the twenty-one-year-old son of friends of mine was found to have bone cancer. His parents had to take him three thousand miles from home, to a hospital in Seattle, in a desperate attempt to have him treated with a new and experimental therapy. When word of their problem got out, some astonishing things began to happen. Service clubs organized fund-raising drives to help pay their expenses. One of Seattle's finest hotels invited them to stay at no charge while the boy was in the hospital; restaurants served them and would not accept their money. The governor of Massachusetts intervened to direct their health insurance company to assume the cost of what some held to be an experimental form of treatment. Some might ask, Why would God permit a twenty-one-year-old to fall ill with cancer? I am inclined to ask, What moves people to respond to tragedy with such generosity and compassion if not God? The skeptic and the agnostic are able to explain the evil in the world by denying God's role in human affairs. But how do they explain the good? Having explained cruelty and crime, how do they explain generosity, kindness, courage, and self-sacrifice, unless God is at work on us the way the sun affects the flower, making it grow and blossom and reveal its most beautiful inner self?

God gives us hope in a way that no human agent can. Among humans, Murphy's Law operates: Anything that can go wrong will. But at the divine level, there is another, opposite law: Anything that should be set right sooner or later will. God is the answer to the question, What is the point of trying to make the world better if problems of war, hunger, injustice, and hatred are so vast and stubborn that I can't even make a dent in them in my lifetime? God assures us, in a way that no mortal can, that what we do not achieve in our lifetime will be completed beyond our lifetime and in part because of what we did in our lifetime. Human beings may be mortal, appearing on earth for just a few years, but God's will is eternal. Ecclesiastes worried, What is the point of all the good I do if I die and all my good deeds are forgotten? The answer is that good deeds are never wasted and not forgotten. What cannot be achieved in one lifetime will happen when one lifetime is joined to another. People who never knew each other in life become partners in making good things happen, because the Eternal God gives their deeds a measure of eternity.

I have stood in the Canadian Rockies and have seen the gorges cut into the mountain rock by flowing streams of water. To the casual observer, it would seem that nothing on earth is harder than rock and nothing easier to divert than water. Yet, over centuries, the water has won the battle, cutting into and reshaping the rock. No one drop of water is stronger than rock, but each one contributed to the ultimate victory.

What questions burdened Ecclesiastes to which God could have been the answer? In the fall of 1952, I was a sophomore at Columbia University. I was too young to vote but old enough to follow the presidential election with interest. Although Dwight Eisenhower was president of Columbia at that time, most of my classmates favored the Democrat, Adlai Stevenson. (At Princeton, Stevenson's alma mater, the students were for Eisenhower.) But what I remember most about the election of 1952 is not that Eisenhower won or that Stevenson lost but that Robert Taft died so soon after it.

For a generation, Senator Robert Taft of Ohio had been the conscience of the Republican party, the embodiment of its principles as an alternative to the New Deal. His lifelong ambition had been to be President of the United States as his father, William Howard Taft, had been. With the Democrats complacent and scandal-ridden after twenty years in office, with an unpopular war in Korea, 1952 looked like his year. But that summer, the Republican party turned to Eisenhower, a war hero to millions of Army veterans and other Americans. Taft died shortly after Eisenhower's inauguration.

I remember that at the time, I found it hard to accept the idea that a man like Taft could be well enough to campaign for the presidency in the summer of 1952 and be terminally ill with cancer a few months later. I began to suspect that there was some connection between the collapse of his lifelong dream and the collapse of his health soon afterward.

How do you go on living when you feel that your whole life has been a failure? When you have to concede that the goal you worked for and dreamed of is out of reach and will never be yours, when you are too old to come up with another lifelong goal and you have nothing to look forward to in your remaining years except being reminded daily of your failure, what is the point of being alive? If, through all of your life, you wanted nothing more than to be a good wife and mother to people you loved, and in mid-life you find yourself divorced or widowed through no fault of your own, or your children have turned out very differently from how you hoped they would, where do you find the strength to keep walking into the future? If your driving dream was to be more successful than your father, to earn more money and achieve higher status so that he would finally have to admit that you had what it took, and now you confront the fact that you will never do it, how do you live with the broken fragments of that dream?

To what question, then, is God the answer? Among other things, He is the answer to, How can you go on living when you feel that your life has been a failure? "For man sees only what is visible, but the Lord sees into the heart." (I Samuel 16:7) Secular human society, man without God, can only judge by results, by achievements. Did you win or did you lose? Did you make it happen or did you fail? Did you show a profit or a deficit? But God alone can judge us on the basis of what we are, not only what we have done. In a secular society, only deeds have value, and so people are worthwhile only if they do things, if they are productive and successful. When a person is killed or crippled in an accident, how do we calculate the harm done to him? We figure his lost earning capacity. Teenagers and old people are problems in our society because they live, breathe, and eat, but they are not productive. They don't *do* anything. A college education is recommended not because it deepens your soul and helps you understand life but because it enhances your earning power. So Eugene Borowitz writes, "We fear growing old lest we no longer be useful, that is, able to do things which show others that we have worth. We equate our value with our performing."

When we cannot measure people by God's standards, we can only evaluate them by human standards: Are they *useful?* The woman who is no longer attractive and has passed her childbearing years and the man who can no longer push himself to surpass his sales quota are no longer useful, and therefore they barely exist as people. But if people see only what is visible, measurable, God sees into the heart. He not only forgives our failures, He sees successes where no one else does, not even we ourselves. Only God can give us credit for the angry words we did not speak, the temptations we resisted, the patience and gentleness little noticed and long forgotten by those around us. Just being human gives us a certain value in His eyes, and trying to live with integrity makes us successful before Him.

God might have said to Robert Taft in 1952, as He may have said to Paul Tsongas in 1984, "So you won't be President. Neither will most people. But look at the very real and substantial achievements of your public and your personal life. They should make you feel successful. Losing the nomination should not make you think of yourself as a failure. But losing faith in yourself because you could only do some of what you wanted in life and not all of it, not being able to keep your victories in perspective because of this defeat—that would be failure."

Eugene Borowitz has written:

> We did not anticipate the possibility of deep or lasting failure. We could not believe that our best ideas might be too small, our plans inadequate, our character mean, our wills perverse. We certainly did not expect that in doing righteousness we might also create evil, sometimes ones so great that they seemed to outweigh the good we had done. The result is not only moral malaise but a time in which, amid the greatest freedom and affluence people have ever known, our common psychiatric problem has shifted from guilt to depression. Knowing our failures, we cannot truly believe in ourselves. We cannot even do the good which lies within our power, because failure has convinced us that nothing we might do is worth anything. If religion could teach secular society to accept failure without becoming paralyzed and to reach for forgiveness without mitigating our sense of responsibility, we might end the dejection and moral lassitude which now suffuse our civilization . . . If religion could restore a sense of personal dignity to our society, it would secure the basis upon which any hope of rebuilding the morale of our civilization must rest. (*Journal of Ecumenical Studies,* Summer 1984)

God redeems us from the sense of failure and the fear of failure because He sees us as no human eyes can see us. Some religions teach that God sees us so clearly that He knows all our shameful thoughts and nasty secrets. I prefer to believe that God sees us so clearly that He knows better than anyone else our wounds and sorrows, the scars on our hearts from having wanted to do more and do better and being told by the world that we never would.

Does it make a difference how I live? Does it make a difference if I am a good, honest, faithful, compassionate person? It does not seem to make a difference to my bank account, or my chances for fame and fortune. But sooner or later, we learn as Ecclesiastes learned that those are not the things that really matter. It matters if we are true to ourselves, to our innate human nature that requires things like honesty and kindness and grows flabby and distorted if we neglect them. It matters if we learn how to share our lives with others, making them and their world different, rather than try to hoard life for ourselves. It matters if we learn to recognize the pleasures of every day, food and work and love and friendship, as encounters with the divine, encounters that teach us not only that God is real but that we are real too. Those things make all the difference.

In the Jewish tradition, we celebrate a holiday every autumn known as Sukkot, the Feast of Tabernacles. It is, in part, an old harvest festival, deriving from a time when the Israelites were farmers and would give thanks every autumn when the harvest had been gathered. In fact, it is the prototype of our American festival of Thanksgiving. And in part, it is a commemoration of God's protecting care over Israel during the forty years in the wilderness between Egypt and the Promised Land.

We celebrate Sukkot by building a small annex to our homes, just a few boards and branches, inviting friends in, and drinking wine and eating fruit in it for the week of the holiday. Sukkot is a celebration of the beauty of things that don't last, the little hut which is so vulnerable to wind and rain (ours regularly collapses a day or two after we put it up) and will be dismantled at week's end; the ripe fruits which will spoil if not picked and eaten right away; the friends who may not be with us for as long as we would wish; and in northern climates, the beauty of the leaves changing color as they begin the process of dying and falling from the trees. Sukkot comes in the fall. Summer is over and sometimes the evenings are already chilly with the first whispers of winter. It comes to tell us that the world is full of good and beautiful things, food and wine, flowers and sunsets and autumn landscapes and good company to share them with, but that we have to enjoy them right away because they will not last. They will not wait for us to finish other things and get around to them. It is a time to "eat our bread in gladness and drink our wine with joy" not despite the fact that life does not go on forever but precisely because of that fact. It is a time to enjoy happiness with those we love and to realize that we are at a time in our lives when enjoying today means more than worrying about tomorrow. It is a time to celebrate the fact that we have finally learned what life is about and how to make the most of it. The special scriptural reading assigned for study in the synagogue during the Feast of Tabernacles is the Book of Ecclesiastes.